Tom Tichenor's Puppets

Tom Tichenor's Puppets

Text, Drawings and Photographs by
TOM TICHENOR

ABINGDON PRESS
NASHVILLE • NEW YORK

ISBN 0-687-42363-5
Library of Congress Catalog Card Number: 76-147304
Printed in the United States of America

11

*To Emma Hayes Wade and Mark Ketterson
and to the memory of another Emma,
my mother,
who was my first assistant,
and my lasting inspiration*

Appreciation to

My aunts—Cora Mitchell, who booked my first "professional" show, and Ruby Tichenor, who has suffered with me through the birth of over 500 puppets and marionettes;

Sara Andrews, Marcelle Workman, and the Children's Division, and Marshall Stewart, director, The Public Library of Nashville;

Marsha Thomas and Rosalyn Olsen, long-time members of my unofficial staff, who started on television with me;

John Lovelady, a gifted puppeteer and staunch friend;

Charles Hunt, Linda Makosky, Gwen Kent, Barbara Bomar, Raymond Tichenor, Joanne McCrichard, and all the others who have given of their time and talent to bring the shows to life;

Barbara Harkins and Lin Folk for making the Story Hours such a pleasure;

Chris Tibbott, who no matter how busy her schedule always found time to paint props and backdrops;

Emma King Woods, who taught me how to model heads and paint backdrops;

WSM-TV, Nashville, where my puppets faced cameras for ten years;

WKNO-TV, Memphis, for three and a half years of creative experience;

Gower Champion for championing a provencial puppeteer and putting my puppets on Broadway;

Lester Lewis, Ruth and Paul Tripp, Alton Alexander and Jack Sumroy for three years with "Birthday House" on WNBC-TV, New York;

Ben Jones for additional photographs and his help and patience with mine;

Tim Palkovic for his helpful suggestions during the writing of this book.

Contents

Introduction

There are many kinds of puppets: rod puppets, shadow puppets, finger puppets, and undoubtedly many others, but my work has been with the most familiar ones, hand puppets and string puppets (better known as marionettes). For those of you just embarking on puppetry this book will offer instructions for making basic puppets and step-by-step suggestions for staging a complete play. Hopefully the experienced puppeteer will find inspiration, perhaps a different way of thinking about the craft, and some fresh ideas.

A puppet must live. His life must come from your fingers and heart whether the puppet is on your hand or on strings. This calls for a special skill and a special feeling. There is great difference between jiggling a marionette all over the stage or flopping a hand puppet to and fro in a frantic frenzy and in working them believably. Wild movement is not to be confused with real animation. By his very nature a puppet cannot be made to act completely realistically. Nor is this always truly desirable anyway. A puppet must be worked in such a manner that you believe in his character and feel that he is alive. This takes practice and more practice, and real love for the art of puppetry.

It has often been said that puppeteering is the dramatic art form in which one person is in complete control. True, the puppeteer usually makes and costumes his own puppets, constructs the props, scenery, and stage, writes the script, directs the show, and, in some cases, even writes the music. But rare is the play that one person can perform alone. It is possible, of course, for one person to do a club act or a specialty number, but a full-length play—that's something else. Assistants are necessary. In some instances they are necessary evils.

Where does one find a helper who will exhibit the skill, the sensitivity, the dependability that a puppet show demands? One searches, digs, prays. When you find someone with these qualities, make him want to stay. Encourage him, let him know he is appreciated; and, above all else, let him share the limelight.

A puppet show is only as good as the puppeteers. I would rather see a play performed beautifully with inferior puppets than see one with gorgeous puppets operated sloppily. What is more disenchanting than seeing a marionette suddenly take wings and fly offstage instead of walking? Or seeing a hand puppet sink inch by inch into quicksand as it crosses the stage?

And while we're on that subject, here is a bit of advice for the director-puppeteer. Once the play begins, forget that you are the director. Concentrate on the puppets you are operating. The moment you try to give directions, by nods, thought waves, or whatever, the puppet you are operating will suffer. A marionette that droops, a hand puppet that freezes—either is sure death to a scene.

Everyone is influenced by what he sees. It is human nature to emulate the things one admires. In my case there were two strong influences: Beatrix Potter and Walt Disney. Through the years their divergent styles have continued to play a part in my creations; but, hopefully, only in an inspirational way. Every true artist develops his own individual style. My medium is cloth—all kinds of cloth and all textures of cloth. The wonderful fake furs available now constantly inspire me to make more animals.

I started out making puppets with heads modeled in paper-mache—the old kind, made with newspapers soaked in water and flour paste that soured. Then I progressed to plastic wood. I would rather forget the hours spent in digging the stuff out of the plaster molds, and in sanding, still never quite getting the smooth face I so much wanted for a princess. One must admit that sculptured heads are more realistic, more elegant, more European. The cloth heads tend to be more stylized and, to my way of thinking, more lovable. It hurts less to see an unrealistic puppet handled inexpertly than to see a miniature manikin stumble about. Perhaps that is why I really prefer animal puppets. Audiences tend to like them no matter what they do or how they do it.

All of this is by way of saying: try all styles, even mix them; be influenced by brilliant artists and by the Muppets and—this I sincerely wish—by the things you see in this book. But don't copy other styles for long. Develop your own interpretation of things you like. Strive to create your own style. Your puppets should be you.

It has been pointed out to me over and over that my puppets seem to have a wistful, half-sad look. This is interpreted to mean that I am a little bit sad behind my smile. Perhaps this is true. One cannot be truly happy when one's potentials have not been realized. But then, what is happiness? Although I have not achieved all my goals, I have spent my life doing the work I like, and not everyone can say that.

My puppets do not look like anyone else's, so they have their individuality. They have a look, create an effect. That effect, that overall appearance, is important in a puppet. For the beginner in puppetry this is a vital thing. It can often be achieved with unskilled efforts. As you progress in the art, you should develop a pride in workmanship. You do not have to put in fine details, as in an antique christening gown, even when your're designing for television. The simple, uncluttered look is best.

Craftsmanship definitely has its place. A puppet should be well made. The best argument for making sturdy puppets is that they will last longer and look good longer. Puppets lead hard lives. In a performance the little actors are subjected to treatment that no human actor could survive.

Too, you never know when a puppet will suddenly shine forth and become a star. If it is not well made, the puppet will soon disintegrate with hard usage. It has been my disappointing experience that a puppet that wears out can seldom be duplicated. The original one gradually takes on a shape and feeling that only time and frequent use can give it.

I am still using puppets made twenty years ago. Poindexter, my faithful hound, has had his teeth capped and his nose slipcovered at least twice. Threads wear out, but his basic construction is still sound. Several attempted duplicates lurk in the cupboards, but they are impostors. The look in the eyes, the way the ears move are just not Poindexter. The original is the one and only, and it will be a sad day when he really does fall apart. That will happen because the fabric turns to dust, not because he was carelessly thrown together.

People frequently want to know what I do with my old puppets. I use them, that's what! Even though my technique and style have changed gradually through the years, I always seem to provide roles for favorite puppets, such as the Prime Minister, created in 1953 for Witchie's first TV series "The Green Cheese Adventure," or Witchie herself, who is still going strong. She made her dramatic stage debut (after all those years in television) in *Christmas at Creepy Castle,* a show created for her in 1968. It ran for a month, and was brought back in 1969 by popular demand. Included as one of the plays in this book, it is an example of a show that plays well and that audiences love, although it undoubtedly breaks every rule of playwrighting.

So you see, it pays to construct your puppets carefully. You may want them around and in usable condition for years to come.

I
MY PUPPET FAMILY

A most important phase of my work has been the Story Hour presentations at the Nashville Public Library. The story sessions have been very simple: no elaborate sets, no tremendous casts of gorgeously gowned puppets. True, the story is the essential factor in these sessions, but the way it is told is our primary concern here. That's where my puppet family comes into the picture. Puppets that are used in such a situation must have well-defined characters and personalities. The audiences must identify with them, react to them, and remember them with affection.

Most puppeteers create one or more puppets that soon become their favorites. They know how these puppets think and how they would react to a situation. The puppets change a bit from time to time, grow in character and feeling, develop their own mannerisms and traits. They become in effect real people.

Naturally I have my favorites, and I'd like to tell you how they began their careers, how they grew and changed. Perhaps this will give you an insight into my approach to puppetry and show you why a "puppet family" is invaluable.

POINDEXTER

Poindexter, a flop-eared hound, was my third hand puppet. For ten years he and a little gnome called Gerome opened every marionette show at the Nashville Public Library with a traditional hide-and-seek game. The slightest variation in this routine ruined the effect. I must admit that doing the same thing every week for that many years was monotonous. However, it was a great help to me in learning why certain things would work and others would not. Poindexter went into television in its early years, debuting on an educational program where his duty was to bolster the courage of frightened teachers appearing before the cameras for the first time.

He went on to be host on cartoon shows, afternoon jungle film shows, and Saturday morning free-for-alls. All this time he remained the mild, rather quiet straight man who made people laugh just by being friendly and looking so funny. In Memphis he hosted a series of fifteen-minute shows for NET called "Tales of Poindexter." When I moved to New York in 1961, poor old Poindexter, at the advanced age of eleven, went into retirement.

In 1969, back in Nashville, I used him in summer Story Hours. He met a quick favorable reaction from the children. He is, after all, a dog, and everybody is supposed to love a dog. But I had lost his personality. As a matter of fact, some of his traits had been given to two other puppets.

That autumn Poindexter joined Felicia Fieldmouse in a routine at the beginning of the regular Story Hour and was a different individual. He was stubborn, a bit aggressive, and much funnier.

At the age of nineteen he was one of five puppets chosen for an ABC-TV Christmas special. I guess you can teach an old dog new tricks. Poindexter may be older, but he wears well. More and more his old brightness shines through. He gets his biggest laugh when he acts surprised at being treated like a dog. Who can say what he would be like today if he had worked steadily instead of spending eight-and-a-half years in retirement?

FELICIA FIELDMOUSE

Felicia Fieldmouse, senior citizen of the troupe, first appeared in 1947 in *Thumbelina*. Many times I have been tempted to destroy this marionette with her cloth head stiffly painted gray with tempera, and her hands shaped like miniature baseball mitts. Now I look upon her as a historical

artifact—positive proof that my work has grown and improved. *Thumbelina* was reworked a few years after the original performance, and Felicia grew much larger, assuming the general look that she has today. She still remained the fieldmouse in the Hans Christian Andersen story, a fluttery little matchmaker who preferred visiting to housekeeping.

In 1958, on her eleventh birthday, she became a hand puppet also, so she could appear in a TV play I had written, *The Churchmouse's Christmas*. At last the real Felicia came forth. She knew what to do and how to do it. No longer a giddy old lady, she was instead a small personage with dignity, poised, and with a fervent desire to be constructive.

In 1964 Felicia began her appearances on WNBC-TV in New York, on "Birthday House" with Paul Tripp. Before the eyes of a million children she continued to grow in character and appeal.

She became mistress of the Puppet Playhouse at the Nashville library early in 1968. From the first day there was no doubt about who was boss. Here was the matriarch, the slapstick comedienne, the clotheshorse, and the world's greatest bad actress, all rolled into one diminutive puppet with mohair head, nylon whiskers, and nose glasses that never fall off.

MARCO POLO BEAR

In 1950 Marco Polo Bear first appeared as a marionette in the annual Christmas show *Jingle the Christmas Brownie*. He strolled in on all fours, a typical polar bear, upsetting Santa's letters, packages, everything. I pondered over a voice to give him. As it happened, I had a cold, so he had a cold. That cold in the nose became his trademark. The next year he became a hand puppet, and was accepted on TV as Witchie's adopted son.

In 1961, in New York, Marco grew to his present size, with movable mouth and hands added. He was instrumental in my landing the television job there. During my audition, Paul Tripp asked Marco questions. Afterwards, Paul said, "He's the first puppet I've talked to who thinks. You see the wheels going around in his head."

Marco's work on "Birthday House" gave him a chance to grow and develop as an individual. He has his own way of looking at things, and

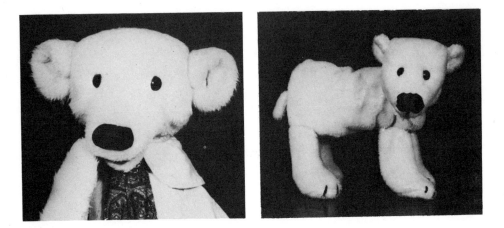

possesses a kind of inner calm. He is a serious actor. For four months he played a dramatic role in one of our Patchwork Playhouse plays, *The Dragon*. He was Peter the Potter, doing scenes with both puppets and people. Not once did anyone question why a polar bear was playing a pottery maker. His sincerity made him quite believable.

In the Story Hours he likes to play multiple roles. He has played each one of the three bears, the three little pigs, and an elephant.

People are always saying that he changes his expression. Actually, he has the blankest expression of any of my puppets. His simplicity of design and expressive attitudes create the illusion. I like to think his inner feelings show through.

Marco Polo Bear is the eternal little boy, with the wisdom of the innocent and the naiveté of the guileless.

WITCHIE

Witchie was created quickly one day in the early fifties to take part in a television skit. She was given a black outfit with the traditional peaked hat, and green yarn hair. A year later—in 1953, to be exact—she appeared in the second program of a summer serial. She took so much

time showing off, that she did not complete her prescribed business for the day. This can easily happen when you are ad-libbing a show. Witchie had to come back on the next program to continue the plot. After that second appearance she was the star of the series. She literally took over! The other puppets were merely her supporting cast. She could salvage any mishap and could do it with humor.

To give her the star treatment, I made a new puppet. This time her hair was made of the then-new Saran, mint green. She joined Poindexter in hosting all sorts of afternoon film shows, on which she wore a remarkable collection of mismatched earrings sent in by her fans.

In 1957 I started commuting to Memphis, where I became Children's Director of the educational station WKNO-TV. Witchie had her third incarnation. There was no more green Saran hair available, so she settled for pink. To go with it, she had a medieval hostess gown of purplish red velvet. For a year she lived in a castle appropriately called Witch-haven. She published a newspaper called Witch-Haven News, and had her patience tried by many cousins. One was a witch who called herself Monticello, and went on archeological digs near the moat, finding "neolithic" coke bottles and "paleolithic" powder puffs. Another cousin was Gertrude Troll, who liked things damp, and grew mushrooms in the carpets. The next year it was with some relief that Witchie journeyed to outer space to become hostess on a space station. All went well until Gertrude Troll arrived for a visit and flooded the lower reactor room so she could go swimming.

All this while Witchie was also doing bit parts in other TV series, just to prove that although a beautiful, successful television star, she was also a humble actress, to whom the size of her role did not matter—as long as she had a beautiful costume. When asked to play the witch in *The Tinderbox*, she replied "I'll do it if my patched cloak is made by Fontana of Rome and my witch hat is as floppy as the ones worn by Garbo." She got the part—and the wardrobe.

Sadly she went into retirement in New York with Poindexter. She had one chance at TV in New York, but they didn't understand her. They had never met a grande dame witch before. They wanted the common garden variety. So she spent her days doing Yoga and her nights chatting with visitors.

Then, in 1967, came her most thrilling moment, her legitimate stage debut at the library in Nashville. She had been born practically on television, but had never acted on stage. Her devoted friend and admirer (guess who) concocted a play just for her: *Christmas at Creepy Castle*. She threw her heart, soul, and broom into the play, and it was so popular that it was brought back by popular demand in 1969.

The second time around, *Christmas at Creepy Castle* was even more fun. Beautiful sets were added, and the production attracted the largest crowd ever to attend a puppet show at the library. The play was strictly ad-lib, with only a traffic pattern posted so the various characters would come in at the right time. It is a true example of a play that grows. Things that happened spontaneously, spur-of-the-moment inspirations, accidents that got a laugh—all were incorporated. And finally it was all written down for this book.

Witchie was no problem at all in her comeback. The years of idleness had no affect on her timing and her spirit. She is one of a kind, and the mistress of all she surveys. Her chief asset is her energy; she radiates vitality. Like most of my characters, she is a contradiction. She's a witch, but not a witch. She's vain and domineering, but sweet and compassionate. She's ugly, but beautiful. She's loud and outgoing, but gentle and retiring. She's an actress to her fingertips—but doesn't have fingers. She's a woman.

DUCKIE

Duckie was made in 1965 to animate a song on TV. A handsome swan was made at the same time. The swan was never again seen on TV, but Duckie returned the next day and became a star. She learned to talk on the air, and once she had started, there was no stopping her. She bears a scar on one wing where she was burned in an abortive rocket-ship blast-off.

Except for her own hair, which she hides under a wig, she considers herself flawlessly beautiful. Her eyes and bill are crooked, but not to her. Her dramatic delivery of lines makes her a welcome addition to any cast. She frequently plays the part of a spoiled little girl. Is that acting?

24

STUMBLEWEED

Stumbleweed is a rambunctious, faded-yellow horse, who describes himself as a golden pimento. He is full of fun and useless schemes.

SHELDON CROCODILE

Sheldon Crocodile likes to play tricks. His voracious appetite turns out to be a fraud when he opens his toothless mouth.

25

OWLFIE

Owlfie doesn't give a hoot what others think. After all, every owl can't be wise—an observation which may prove he is smarter than he thinks he is.

GRISWOLD

Griswold is a young grizzly bear who never says anything. His reactions are as expressive as words. He is the only puppet who is never put away. He sits in my livingroom in his own little Morris chair, observing, looking friendly. Most visitors think this is his home, not mine. He never performs professionally. He is more teddy bear than puppet.

GRIZELDA

Grizelda is Griswold's little sister. For two years she appeared on educational TV with a Storybook Princess. She sat beside the Princess' throne

on her own little stool, following the lines of the story as the Princess
read from the book. She is ever the proper lady. She has the knack of
looking alive while doing nothing. A puppet that is completely inanimate
is merely a stuffed toy. Grizelda sighs quietly, breathes deeply at times,
and does all the subtly human things that most puppets never do. Yet
she never distracts from the storyteller. This ability alone would endear

Griswold *Grizelda*

27

her to any costar, but she has talent too. She is a poetess, who has composed such deathless lines as:

> I went for a walk
> Down by the trees,
> I saw a fox
> Eating pimento cheese.

I know so well how my puppet family members think, I don't have to stop to figure out their actions. They seem to act independently of me. Sometimes they surprise me as much as the audience.

These puppets have become such strong personalities that I speak of them as if they were really alive. In planning sessions they are referred to the same as any other actors. People are sometimes unnerved by my attitude, at least at first. They want to know how I can talk that way about the puppets and still pack them in bags, stick pins in them, and treat them as casually as I would a rag doll. It's simple: the physical puppets are products of my craftsmanship; their personalities are a living part of my mind and hands. When I put myself inside them, they come alive.

I always put the puppets away after a performance. Seeing them strewn about distracts me—but that is not the main reason I prefer them out of sight. I find it disturbing when a stranger walks in and puts his hand in my very personal puppets. He invariably distorts the puppet's face, turning him into a grotesque gargoyle. I try to hide my feelings, but it's a painful experience. The only comparison I can make is with the way parents would feel if they saw someone pull their child's ears and nose and then carelessly drop the child on the floor. And you would be amazed at how often I have to pick the puppets up from the floor to keep people from stepping on them.

For the most part, people are very considerate, and respect the vulnerability of puppets. But for those who are not, the best solution is the one we use after the Story hour. The puppets stay in the Puppet Playhouse, where no one can touch them, and I bring out one designed expressly to be touched by visitors.

II
THE STORY HOUR WITH PUPPETS

A Story Hour with puppets definitely needs a human story-teller out front. A puppet play can be given without any such person, for that is a straight dramatic performance. A Story Hour is a different thing. By its very nature it needs to be intimate and personal. Its success depends on the relationship established between the storyteller and the children sitting before him. Puppets can enhance this relationship greatly. But a puppet trying to tell a story by itself cannot hold the children's attention as strongly. The eye-to-eye contact is necessary.

The storyteller and the puppeteer must develop a way of working together. They must develop a rare rapport that enables them to chat back and forth, improvising dialogue, but without stepping on each other's lines or talking at the same time. Some people can do this instinctively. Others can achieve it with practice. Those who can't—well, they had better work alone. Nothing is more annoying to the performers or the audience than two people talking at the same time, obscuring every sentence and meaning.

In learning to work as a team, it helps to concentrate very hard. Listen

The storyteller and Marco Polo Bear (in the Puppet Playhouse) in the Story Room, Nashville Public Library

to what is being said and try to sense when you should speak. Many people do not really listen, especially when they have done the same routine many times before. They automatically say their lines without hearing what is going on in the room. Performers should never become that bored or matter-of-fact.

Each audience reacts differently, be it ever so subtly. The storyteller and puppeteer must gear their dialogue and responses to the audience's reactions. When a child beats you to a punch line, you not only need to be listening, but to be thinking ahead.

Stories can be told in a bare room with no atmosphere except what the storyteller creates. Almost everyone can recall hearing a ghost story around a campfire; now that is real atmosphere. I was privileged to design the Story Room in the Public Library of Metropolitan Nashville and Davidson County. It has a warm, friendly atmosphere that is conducive to a good Story Hour. It helps to set a receptive mood. Our Story Room has books because it is in a library. And these are special books, books of fairy tales, folklore, poetry, and Christmas stories. There are shadow boxes with miniature scenes; the furniture was designed and made just for the room. No other spot in the library has what this place has, and purposely so. It is special. People like to go in and visit, or just sit and soak up the welcome. There is a magic mirror on a secret door, a jewel-encrusted birthday chair, and some antique copper and brassware.

Then, when it is story time the room comes to life. The storyteller appears, as if by magic, trhough the secret door. The doors of the Puppet Playhouse open, and in the midst of this old-fashioned world something happens. It is Now! It is the world of make-believe relating to today.

The Playhouse is our proof that imagination has a valid place in the life of everyone, child and grownup. Where do our inventions come from? They had their start in someone's imagination. Where do our great books come from? Or the marvelous buildings throughout the ages? From someone's imagination.

Everything stems from a healthy imagination. Puppets are pure make-believe. We never tell anyone that the puppets are alive. The storyteller always ends the visit by saying that the puppets needed someone to make them work, and out I come. But when I'm performing I throw my entire being into creating the illusion that the puppets are living, thinking creatures. That's what puppeteering is all about. And puppets can add an extra dimension to the Story Hour.

The Puppet Playhouse is extremely small. I sit inside it on a tiny stool with puppets hanging all about me. The double doors open up to form a stage that is only 18 x 20 inches, but is big enough for a puppet as large as Marco Polo Bear.

THE REGULAR STORY HOUR

When I returned to Nashville at the end of 1967 after a seven-year stay in New York, I joined the library Story Hour in mid-session. Because the library storytellers had told stories without puppets—and had told

Tom Tichenor backstage at the Puppet Playhouse

them beautifully—I had to fit my puppets into the established routine and adjust them to stories which had been previously selected for the season. School groups, usually preschoolers, were scheduled for six story hours a week.

During those first months, the storyteller and I learned what worked best, how the puppets could add the most, the things that did not work, in short, how to plan for the next season. We wanted to achieve more than an ordinary story hour; we wanted to provide an experience that would both entertain and inspire.

Felicia Fieldmouse makes a tentative entrance

Word quickly spread that the puppets were back in town. Older classes came, and we started having a demonstration Story Hour for college classes. In the question-and-answer sessions teachers and librarians always want to know how we work up the little routines we use before and between stories. We tell them that actually they seem to evolve from a small beginning and grow and grow. I'll illustrate with Felicia's routine as it was during those first months.

The storyteller would knock on the Puppet Playhouse doors. Felicia would open them and come out with her broom. She would show surprise that the guests were already there and she had not swept the porch, which she would proceed to do with gusto. When she had finished, she would leave, and Marco would appear. For weeks we heard the children ask Marco, "Where is your mother?" He never answered, because no mention had ever been made of his mother. One day a little voice asked, "Where is your mother mouse?" Then we knew. Felicia's sweeping, plus her attitude, had established her as the mother figure. The children seemed to want to see more of her.

The second season Felicia swept and pointed out that her broom was made of feathers so she could sweep the spider webs. She said, "I don't want to make the spiders mad." "Oh, you just tickle them a little bit?" "Yes, it's better to make spiders laugh than to make them angry."

Since we needed an excuse to bring her back later, she excused herself by saying she had to go to the dry cleaners to get her new dress, the orange one. The storyteller extracted a promise that she would put it on and come back so everyone could see it. On cold or rainy days she would put on her patched, hooded cape and be on her way. Her return at the end of the Story Hour was always a hit because of her beautiful orange dress with feathers.

The third season Felicia opened the doors without her broom in hand. Poindexter, faithful dog that he is, would bring it to her. Then he parked himself on the left side of the stage and refused to move so she could sweep there. Just when her temper was ready to show itself, she had an idea. She would trick him into moving. She pretended that her side of the stage was the best. At first, Poindexter was satisfied with his place. But the more she raved about her place and all its advantages, the more he wanted to be there. He shouted, "I want to stay there!" She jumped up and said "Don't raise your voice to me. Now, sit!" She pushed him down.

"Sit! What does she think I am, a dog?" (This always drew a big laugh for Poindexter.) But Felicia continued to rave about her special place. It was more than Poindexter could stand. He said to the audience, "I know. I'll growl at her," which he proceeded to do most fiercely. She jumped, and pushed him away, saying "Don't growl at me." Once she had settled herself again, he returned with a half growl. Again she warned him and pushed him away. The third time he gave a tiny little growl. Felicia hopped up, saying, "Don't even think about growling. Now, stay!" She pushed him down. He turned to the audience, "There she goes with that dog business again."

At last, in desperation, he begged, "Please let me stay there." Since he asked so nicely she let him, and so he moved and she could sweep the floor. When she finished, he did not want to take the broom back to the broom closet for her, so she resorted to more trickery. "You simply have to know how to handle a dog," she explained with feminine logic. She tickled his nose with her feather broom. Naturally he sneezed (away from the audience, of course—an object lesson in manners). She exclaimed, "Poindexter, are you catching cold? I had better look at your throat. Open wide and say 'ahhh'." He did, and she put the broom in his mouth. His protests were met with "Don't talk with your mouth full, dear. It's impolite." Thus grew the broom business.

And in similar fashion so did Felicia's dress-up routine. When it was time to dash to the cleaners she couldn't find her old straw hat. It had previously been placed near the fireplace where the children could spot it. The storyteller put the hat on Felicia's head and told her to be careful going down the stairs. She started down daintily, and fell with a little shriek. Her hat flew out into the audience. The children all gasped in surprise. She never said "Ouch" nor did she cry, so she was obviously not hurt. The hat was replaced on her head, she promised not to fall. She started down, and stopped just before her ears were out of sight. "See! I didn't fall." All the while she was running back up the steps. She gave a third farewell and started down again. You guessed it, she fell. The hat flew out into the audience. The children were just as surprised as before. But Felicia was not to be outdone by the stairs. She decided to take the elevator down. She pushed an imaginary button and slowly disappeared from view.

When she returned later, in her fine dress, she was filled with joy. She reported that a lovely lady had said to her, "I'd love to have you for lunch, meow. I'll be over for you at noon, meow." You can imagine the consternation this brought forth from the audience. All ended well as she carefully locked her doors.

The children who had seen the routines a season before loved the new turns the familiar had taken. Yet the situations were complete so newcomers could enjoy them with no previous reference. You can be as ridiculous as you wish as long as there is a bit of reason to it. I try to base the fun on a situation that is identifiable with the audience. Your flights of fantasy can soar to any extreme as long as your feet are on the ground.

Marco Polo Bear explains his perpetual ("that means I have it all the time") cold in the nose by saying that he is from the North Pole. His nasal stoppage has met with no disapproval from speech therapists, because it is caused by a cold—something that everyone has had—and is not a speech defect. This distinction is something to keep in mind when giving a voice to a puppet. Even a suggestion that you are making fun of a stutter or stammer can cause much ill will. If you make a character talk funny because he is frightened, that is one thing. To try for laughs from something a person cannot help is another. In Marco's case, he does not even know that he sounds different. He once set himself up as Duckie's speech teacher.

Marco's duty is to lead the storyteller into the stories. Often he will want to help by acting out parts. At times he will merely pantomine the action while the storyteller does the voices. Other times he will sit and listen along with the children. He can help set the mood by saying, "I'll be as quiet as a mouse. I will even be as quiet as two mice. That's twice as quiet." To which the storyteller adds, "And I'll bet the boys and girls can be as quiet as three mice [whispering], can't you?" The children answer in whispers. Puppets can lead the way oftimes more effectively than a grownup.

Children love to talk directly to Marco. He asks them riddles and keeps score of their answers. They love his mock distress when they guess most of the answers. He always throws them kisses when he leaves, and they always return the affection.

Ex Libris the Bookworm comes out, as it were, to do the commercial.

He loves the words in books. In fact, he eats the words with his eyes. The storyteller is horrified, "You eat the books?" "No, no," he replies, "we never chew the pages, or scribble on them or tear them, do we? Never. When I say I eat words with my eyes, I mean I—read." He loves to eat the pictures with his eyes too. Except when there is too much purple. Too much purple gives him a tummy ache, and his tummy goes from his chin to the tip of his tail. That is a very long tummy ache. It is good for a puppet to have a good exit line. Ex Libris (called Ex for short) uses this: "If I wave goodbye, will you wave back? (They will) I'll bet you can't do this!" He proceeds to wave with his tail. It is amazing how many children think they can!

Ex Libris is worked cross-handed, with the right hand in his head, the left in his tail. On a long surface he can move along as any proper worm should, and Ex is very proper. After all, he lives in a library and eats many a book with his eyes.

Sheldon Crocodile is the buffoon, much in the traditional Punch-and-Judy manner. He does a "Where is he?" hide-and-seek routine with Skunkie, followed by his famous circus trick. He pretends he is a lion, and the skunk puts his head in the lion's mouth. Sheldon teases the audience with the threat of biting Skunkie, and by the time he actually holds the skunk's head no one ever screams. He immediately releases the skunk, who leans against him and pats him. Sheldon explains that he would never hurt the skunk, because they are friends. Skunkie shows his agreement by kissing the crocodile's long nose again and again.

My puppets never hurt each other, even in fun. Action and violence are not synonymous. An overdose of quietness can be dull, so laughter is a welcome release. But the storyteller must always be in control of the audience and not allow levity to become an uproar. Stories cannot be told in an atmosphere of bedlam.

Only by practice and the cultivation of instinct can you learn the simple ways to change routines and stories for use with different age groups. Usually the adaptation is accomplished by the character's own approach to the situation. When Marco is identifying with adults, he plays a wee baby in a way that makes grownups roar with laughter. For preschoolers he sees the baby as a kindergartner does.

In planning the Story Hour for a new season, we gather together many possible stories. The storyteller is more familiar with the newest books than I am. We select the stories that will give the puppets the best opportunities for participation and have the most dramatic possibilities, being always mindful of the age groups that dominate our attendance.

With over three hundred hand puppets to use in casting, it might seem that story selection would be no problem at all. But the Story Hour presentation is not a play: it is making a story come to life; it is a visit with a charming storyteller and friendly puppets, who really are old friends.

At the end of each Story Hour the storyteller calls me to come from the Puppet Playhouse. I bring a red sock, which the children recognize as an ordinary sock. I tell them it is a kind of puppet, one they can make themselves. I slip it on my hand, and they discover two white-button eyes, a scrap of furry hair, and a mouth that is held in place with two stitches. I call the puppet "Mr. Red Sock." He imitates dogs and cats, and tries to bite the children's fingers. Somehow, when children put on a mouth puppet, they want to bite someone, and, if someone else has the mouth puppet, the children want it to bite them. So I tell the children that Mr. Red Sock will be waiting by the door as they leave and will gladly taste their fingers if they so wish. They usually do. Some children even want their ears, noses, and hair tasted. Mr. Red Sock is never aggressive with shy children. They are reminded that he has no teeth to hurt them, and that it is really only my hand inside him. It's funny how many forget that.

Because a sock puppet is so easy to make and such uncomplicated fun to work, it has been chosen to lead off the section on how to make puppets. (See page 46.)

CREATIVE DRAMATICS FOR THE STORY HOUR

During the summer the attendance for the Story Hour jumps to astronomical proportions. The cozy Story Room cannot begin to hold the children (and grownups! They feel cheated when they cannot see and hear what's going on). The group moves into the library auditorium. The Puppet Playhouse looks insignificant on the big stage, so we use a larger puppet stage.

Gone is the intimacy of the quiet Story Hour with a small group. This calls for something with a bigger scope. Yet one cannot come up with a new and elaborate production every week. The problem had to be faced that first summer. The storyteller and I listed our assets:

1. easy rapport between storyteller, puppets, and audience
2. ability to improvise
3. a set of well-known puppets with distinct personalities
4. a daring born of urgency.

We decided to do Creative Dramatics with the puppets. Let them play all the parts the way children would do it. It would work only if the puppets could be themselves, even when acting. It turned out that this was the least of our worries. Each puppet has his own approach to acting, and therein lies the fun.

The puppets prepare for the plays as the audience watches. The story-teller helps Felicia into her costume. After much discussion with Duckie over which one will be the heroine, Felicia wins out, because she has more costumes and a long blond wig that is almost pink.

The stories proceed without rehearsal. The audiences enjoy the "let's-pretend" situation. There is little scenery, if any. Sometimes there are props, but full imagination is called upon. The storyteller is of tremendous importance in helping create the illusions and in bridging parts of the stories that are impossible to dramatize.

These performances—and that is what they really are—demand more spontaneous wit and quick thinking than a regular Story Hour. When you repeat the same stories and bits of business several times a week for two or three months, you have a chance to polish your act. When it is being done one time only, and without rehearsal, with the audience seeing it all happen right then and there, the air is filled with excitement. You could almost charge a battery from the electricity in the air.

What a delightfully smug feeling you have if you present a story successfully; how you bask in the glow of your own cleverness. But there is always the chance that you may fall on your face and die a thousand deaths in five minutes, because it doesn't come off. Therefore it is essential that you know your stories thoroughly. How human and natural for you to wait and skim through the story a moment before curtain time, but how likely to be courting disaster. I am speaking from sad experience. Read the story carefully before scheduling it.

We try to have three stories on every summer program. The publicity releases have to go out two months in advance. In our attempt to include fresh material we dig into old editions of fairy tales and sometimes come up with little-known gems. Sometimes we fail. What may sound good in the first two pages (so good that we include it on our list saying "we'll read the rest of it later") may turn out to be boringly repetitious, grotesque to the point of nausea, or totally without humor. We were thus entrapped by a tale with the enticing title "The Enchanted Pig." The storyteller and I were at once intrigued by the possibility of Felicia's playing the title role. We neglected to read the entire story before the morning of the Story Hour. As luck would have it, the sound system acted up and repairing it took all our spare time. Skimming through the story hastily at the last minute, we discovered that it was much too long, the pig had practically nothing to do in it, and the hero did everything, including having to chop off his finger to complete a bone ladder in order to reach the ending that we thought would never come. "The Enchanted Pig" has become our synonym for disaster. It taught us that there is no substitute for proper preparation.

Try to include one familiar story in every program of this kind. It is always fun when everyone knows the plot. It makes the strange casting more humorous, and the audience can help keep the characters on the right track.

Felicia Fieldmouse always plays the Country Mouse. When Sheldon appears as the City Mouse, everyone laughs, but he plays his part quite seriously. Felicia, being a real mouse, obviously must act her role. She speaks her lines as if she had memorized them. The closer the role to her own identity, the less natural she is in the part. This happens instinctively, and it was only after I had observed it for years that it was explained to me. As an actress Felicia is funny only when she is acting, therefore she must never let the audience confuse her with the part she is playing. Left to their own devices, puppets usually take proper care of things. Just beware of enchanted pigs!

Rhythm bands used with puppets are fun, but only when a piano and pianist are available. Time and again we have tried using records, and it never works. Felicia conducts the band. Squirrels and chipmunks play the drums, pots, pans, cans, and such. Chippie Chipmunk is entrusted with the string of giant jingle bells. He invariably gets carried away with the wonderful sound and ruins everything. Naturally this tries Felicia's patience, and brings on confrontations, threats, promises, and pretended remorse. All ends well with the audience clapping in rhythm. A rhythm band is a good opener for a Creative Dramatic Story Hour. We happened to try it one morning. Chippie fell under the spell of the bells and off we went. Most good routines seem to just happen, and then to grow of their own accord. What works for one puppeteer may be awkward for another. Don't be upset if you can't do what you saw someone do on a TV show. It is much more fun to be original.

When puppets pantomine to records, keep the numbers short. It is tiresome to see a puppet repeat the same movement over and over. If you are stuck with a long record keep the puppet moving.

Use a sound system when performing in a large place. Dialogue must be heard. Learn to use a microphone properly. Don't ever scream into it; be kind to your audience's ears. Test the sound equipment before the doors are opened. Arrange for someone in the rear of the auditorium to come back stage during the performance and tell you if the volume needs changing.

Play to all the audience, not just one section. Give everyone a chance to see the puppets' faces. This may be hard on your fingers and wrists, but if you're comfortable you're not puppeteering.

Keep scene changes as brief as possible. Avoid complicated scenery and props. Ofttimes it is more practical to suggest a setting than to depict it completely.

In the regular Story Hour I work only with a storyteller. In the Creative Dramatic Story Hour I have a puppeteer assistant (sometimes referred to as a partner in crime), and on occasion, two assistants. They are always experienced puppeteers with whom I have complete rapport. You can act* (puppeteers do act, you know) in a regular play with

---

* When the Obraztsov Puppets appeared in New York, I had the pleasure of seeing a performance of *Aladdin* from backstage. The puppeteers were working with emotion in their faces and bodies. At intermission I remarked about this to Sergei Obraztsov himself. He said that if he were given a good actor, he could make him into an excellent puppeteer; but given someone who could manipulate a puppet but could not act, he could never make a good puppeteer.

When I visited the Puppet Theatre in Copenhagen, I was allowed to see from backstage their rod-puppet version of *Puss in Boots*. The puppeteers were all actors. They took off their sandals and worked barefoot, and in the musical number they themselves danced. Needless to say, the puppets were dancing beautifully over their heads.

It takes more than two hands and a puppet to make a puppeteer, and it takes a real puppeteer to make a performance.

someone you do not like, or are not completely in tune with, even though this is never a desirable situation. But to do creative dramatics you need more than that. You need to sense what the other puppeteer is thinking, almost know what he is going to do or not do. You must have a sort of mental cooperation coupled with dramatic skill.

I tell new assistants or apprentices that I demand absolute obedience. This sounds dictatorial and pretentious, and maybe it is. But this is the only way they can learn certain attitudes and styles of performing. An example: Mark was fourteen and puppeteering in his very first creative dramatic performance. We were in the middle of *Rumpelstiltskin*. The storyteller said, "After the miller maid had been queen for a year, a son was born." Felicia (naturally) said, "He is such a handsome baby prince." I whispered to Mark, "Bring up the frog." He did, and the audience laughed. Felicia looked at the frog, turned to the front, and said, "He's not quite as handsome as I remembered." The audience laughed again. The frog blurped, and got a third laugh.

Afterwards I explained to Mark that this demonstrated what I meant by blind obedience. During a performance, ideas pop into my head, such as using the frog for the baby prince. Mark put his hand in the frog and had him onstage in a second. We caught the magic moment. Two seconds' delay and it would have been too late. Mark did not say "Huh?" or ask "Why?" or "What for?" He did what I told him to do. And he added his own touch with the frog sound, building laugh on top of laugh. Mark always listens. He never daydreams in the middle of a performance. He learned to trust me more quickly than others have. He knows I will never call a character onstage and leave him there, while the puppeteer wonders what it's all about. Even puppets can become embarrassed. My puppet will tell why the new character is there and even what is expected of it. When your assistant can toss you an appropriate line to build on, then you know that his days of apprenticeship are over.

In that very same performance of *Rumpelstiltskin* Felicia broke one of the oldest theater rules not once, but several times. She stepped out of character, not that she was ever very far into it. The miller maid had to cry a great deal. No method actress, Felicia. She simply said rather bluntly, "Boo-hoo, boo-hoo." Then she turned to the audience, "Did you ever hear such wonderful crying?" Later on she interrupted her crying to say, "Doesn't my beautiful crying just break your heart?" The king answered, "It certainly does."

I am thoroughly convinced that Felicia knows what she is doing every moment. In improvisational performances she is herself, no matter what she does. It seems she will do anything for a laugh. You are convinced that she really is a dreadful actress with no talent at all. Then she will play the mother in "Jack and the Beanstalk" so fervently that you're positive she has been taking acting lessons. But even then she seems to know exactly when to give melodramatic reading to a line.

I would wish every puppeteer had a Felicia Fieldmouse counterpart. She certainly makes life easier, more interesting, and lots more fun.

I hope you can understand why I encourage you to develop your own puppet "family." You can do plays without them, and I suppose you could do a Story Hour without them. But they wouldn't be quite the same.

III
HAND PUPPETS

Hand puppets are called by different names: glove puppets, fist puppets, and so on, but the one thing they all have in common is that they are worked with hands inside them. They can be beautiful, whimsical or ugly; above all else they must be flexible.

There are no set rules on materials or construction. I prefer cloth heads stuffed with cotton. Hand puppets are never completely comfortable to the puppeteer's hand; one may hope only to make them as bearable and wearable as possible. I have tried heads of plastic wood, paper mache, egg shells, potatoes, sawdust—the list could go on almost forever—and I always return to cloth.

In the appearance of puppets, I strive for lovableness. With animals this seems to come about almost automatically. Perhaps it is the fur cloth; most people seem to want to touch animal puppets. Part of it is in the eyes.

When the first look, the puppet's first appearance, gets an appreciative response half the battle is won.

SOCK PUPPETS

The very simplest hand puppet is one made from a sock. The sock should fit the hand snugly. Orlon stretch socks work nicely, and any color will do. You might try making your first puppet from a worn sock.

Pull the sock on your hand with the heel on top. With your other hand tuck the toe in between your thumb and other fingers to form the mouth. Have someone fasten tiny safety pins in the sides of the mouth. You will notice the upper jaw is wider than the lower jaw. This gives you better control. Take the sock off carefully and sew the mouth firmly before removing the safety pins. I would advise against lining the mouth with felt. The more flexible the mouth, the more expressive it is.

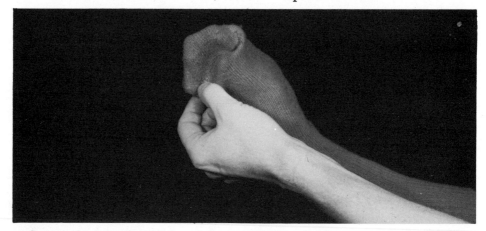

Sew on buttons for eyes, or glue on pieces of felt, or use both. Without a nose the sock puppet can be a snake, or a dragon, or just a "thing." With a chenille ball glued or sewed on, it can be come a person or an animal, depending on the placement of the nose.

Add a snip of fur or fur cloth, some yarn hair, some ears, or a shaggy lion's mane.

There is really no end of fun-characters possible with this easiest-to-make puppet. It can be completed and on the puppeteer's hand in ten minutes or less. Even a very young child can work it, yet it is capable of sophisticated attitudes that will amuse adults.

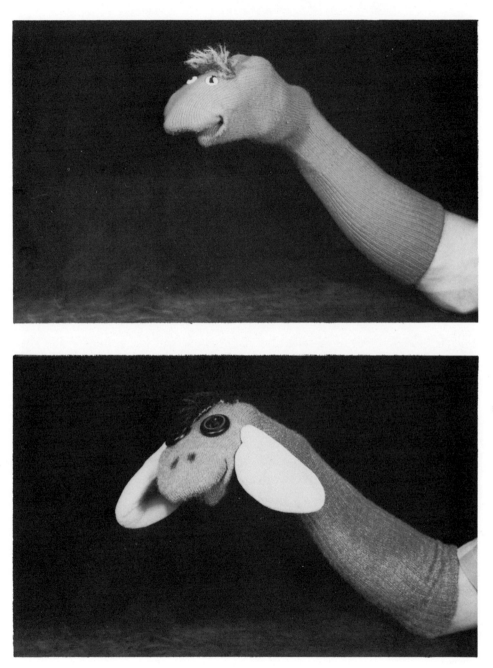

CLOTH PUPPETS

THE HEAD. It is necessary to sew to make cloth puppets. Some may protest that they cannot sew, but costumes have to be sewn no matter what the puppet is made of, so no excuses, please.

There are many advantages to using a cloth head. It can be started and completed without waiting (as with paper-mache or plastic wood) for drying time. The firm, cotton stuffing inside is much more comfortable on the finger than a cardboard tube or a hollow shell. A cloth head of reasonable size is light in weight. The wig can be sewed or pinned on it easily. The head is sewed directly to the body without the hard neck-edge that is found on modeled heads. Hats and headdresses can be pinned easily to the cloth head. This latter feature comes in handy when you create a puppet that is popular and plays many parts.

Use a long needle with an eye sufficiently large to accommodate the thread. If you are working with a large head, a mattress needle will be needed.

A well-made cloth head will take hard usage and last a long time. The main precautions are to keep the cloth off the floor and to avoid handling it with wet or sticky hands. This is good advice for any kind of puppet.

Use peach-colored broadcloth—not pink or orange—for the head. Sew the darts first, using a small stitch. Sew the two sides together, leaving

See patterns, pages 56, 57

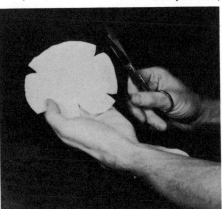 

the top open. Turn and stuff firmly with cotton. As you push in the cotton, take care to avoid lumps and bumps. Fold the top of the head in place and pin down. Sew it securely, taking care to keep the folds from running down onto the face. At the bottom of the head, just to the back of the seam, cut a slit wide enough for the forefinger to go in. By cutting back of the seam you'll make the head jut out just a bit, suggesting a chin. Naturally you have selected the smoothest side for the face.

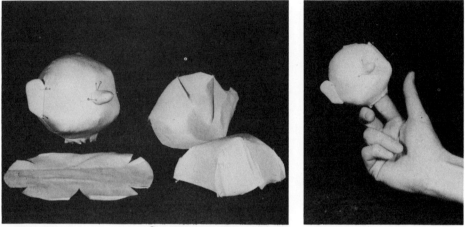

See patterns, pages 56, 57

Now you are ready to make the finger hole in the cotton. Use scissors with sharp points to make the hole. I take an old pair of scissors and, after pushing them into the cotton, pull the handles apart. This makes the hole bigger deep inside the head. Turn the scissors a bit and repeat this. If the hole is too big, the head will slip off the finger during an active scene. If the cotton is too tight, it will cut off the circulation in the finger, and that's no fun. Someone gave me an aluminum cigar case that is dandy for getting the finger hole exactly the right size.

Sew and stuff the nose, pin it in place, and sew it on, going around it with small stitches. Then go round again, this time stitching in between the first stitches. The nose should be placed just below the center of the head.

49

Remember that a person's eyes are placed halfway between the top of the head and the bottom of the chin. Most beginners put the eyes too near the top of the head, creating strange, foreheadless creatures. This is the way very young children draw people. It may be effective for certain characters, but not for ordinary people. Big eyes look innocent. Curve the bottom lines down, and the eyes will have a smile.

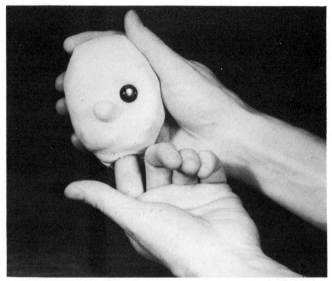

Leave room between the eyes for the puppeteer's finger

For simple eyes on stylized faces use black or colored shank buttons, the kind with a hole on the back. Run the thread from the back of the head through the button and back out again. Pull the thread tightly so the button sinks slightly into the face. This gives modeling to the face. Do not pull the thread so tight that the button makes deep wrinkles in the cloth.

For painted eyes the process is much the same, only it involves more work. Draw the shape of the eyes, not too close together. With black button thread stitch through from the back of the head, starting at the inner corner of the eye. With 1/4-inch stitches go around the eye, pulling it in slightly. I find that as I stitch around the eye I tend to pull the thread a bit more, so that by the time it comes back to the inner corner, the first stitch looks loose. I pull it by the knot until the stitches match, then tie it to the other end, and whip the thread down securely before cutting. Do not continue this thread over to the other eye. You must leave room between the eyes for the puppeteer's finger inside the head.

Once the eyes have been properly indented, they can be painted with acrylic paints. I like a good black line all around the eye, the line a bit

thicker at the top of the eye. Usually, on all but the very smallest children, I paint an eyelid line.

I often sew a shiny black button, or glue a black sequin, in the center of a painted eye to give it a real sparkle.

Of course you can merely paint eyes on the stuffed head, or cut them from felt and glue them on without all the sewing effort. It depends on the "look" you want. Eyes are the telling part of a face. Be certain that they are appropriate for the character, and can be seen from a distance.

Bald Heads can be made by rounding the head pattern at the top to match the bottom, darts and all, then sewing all the way around. Cut a slit across the center of one side for turning and stuffing. When the head is stuffed and the slit sewed up, the seam will be covered by the hair. Make the head wider for a fat man. For a skinny, bald man use the profile head.

Profile Heads are just that. The seam runs down the center of the face. A small stitch on the sewing machine minimizes the line. This type head is ideal for witches or anyone who needs a slender or bony face and sharp features. Leave the neck open. By stuffing the head carefully you can make the brows stick out over the eyes, and the cheekbones very prominent, and even give a suggestion of a jawbone. It is not as easy to stuff this kind of head as the other, but you will find that in pushing the cotton in you have automatically made a finger hole which only needs shaping up.

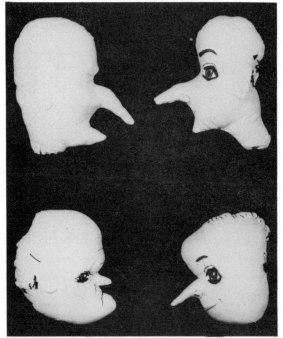

Grotesque or plain profile heads may be cut and sewn to suit any puppeteer's needs

WIGS. Yarn is still one of the most satisfactory materials for hair. It can be sewed directly to the cloth head. Floppy hair is good for boys and happy-go-lucky characters. Sew on a layer of yarn to cover all the scalp. Then add the floppy part, sewing it down the center of the head or across the top from side to side. Leave the ends free to fall where they may.

When you do not have quite enough yarn, cover the scalp with felt or a scrap of cloth the color of the hair yarn. This will enable you to spread out the yarn without giving the appearance of thinning hair.

Beaver fur is good for a man's close-cropped hair. Long fur can create an exotic effect. A scrap of sheepskin makes a curly top for a little boy.

Fur cloth is preferable to real fur most of the time since it wears better. Orlon fur cloth makes great beards, moustaches, and wigs. The grey and white, long-pile fur cloths are superb for old men, dwarfs, and Santa Claus.

Doll wigs can be attractive; however, they are always expensive. The shiny one often are quite heavy, and the mohair wigs tend to go wild after a bit of tossing around. I have one princess who sports real hair—beautiful, naturally curly, auburn locks. She is very conceited, though.

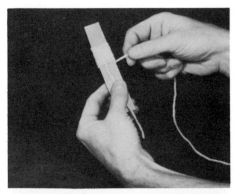

Making a sausage curl

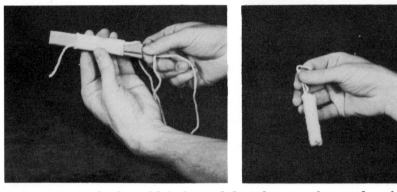

Sausage curls for old-fashioned hairdos can be made of yarn with the aid of a tongue depressor. Let about two inches of yarn extend from the end as you hold it down on the stick. Wind the yarn around the stick carefully. When you reach the other end, measure off about twelve inches before cutting. Thread this in a large needle and run it through the yarn to the other end. Take care to go through every row of yarn. Turn the stick over. Run the needle down the curl and back up again. Take the needle off the thread. Tie the loose ends together. Leave an inch of yarn on the ends when you trim off the excess. Push the loose ends down into the curl when you have slipped it off the tongue depressor. Sew this end to the yarn wig, loosely enough so it will move naturally. Curls made this way can be washed and used over and over again without losing their original shapes. Three can be sewn to one side for a coquettish effect, or a row can be sewn all around the head.

BODIES. The body of a hand puppet is usually its costume. For costume changes in a show you really need as many duplicate puppets as there are changes. There simply is not time to change clothes during or between acts. Long intermissions make for dreary shows.

Sew the peach-colored hands on the sleeves of the waist before sewing the front to the back. If the wrists are to be trimmed with lace or braid, there is an easy way to do it. Sew the front to the back starting at the neck, but stopping before sewing around the hand. Stop halfway down the hand. This will allow you to flatten out the sleeve on the machine and

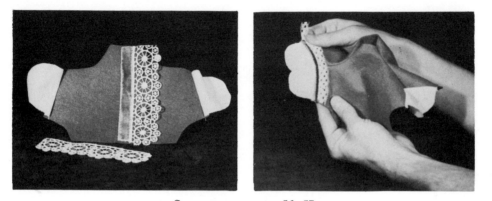

See patterns, pages 56, 57

sew the trim on while it is flat. Then sew the rest of the hand and down to the waistline.

Hands with fingers are difficult to make. Although some people consider them a necessity for realism, I find they hinder movement to a greater degree than they enhance appearance. Puppet fingers usually extend far beyond the puppeteer's fingers. Consequently, he ends up flopping such hands the way a seal does its flippers, or waving them up and down like a semaphore. Fingers make a puppet pick up things with its wrists, while its hands do their awkward nothing. Picking up things is the one business hand puppets do best, and they can be made to do this most easily when the puppeteer's fingers reach the tips of the puppet's hands.

BASIC HEAD FOR PEOPLE PUPPETS

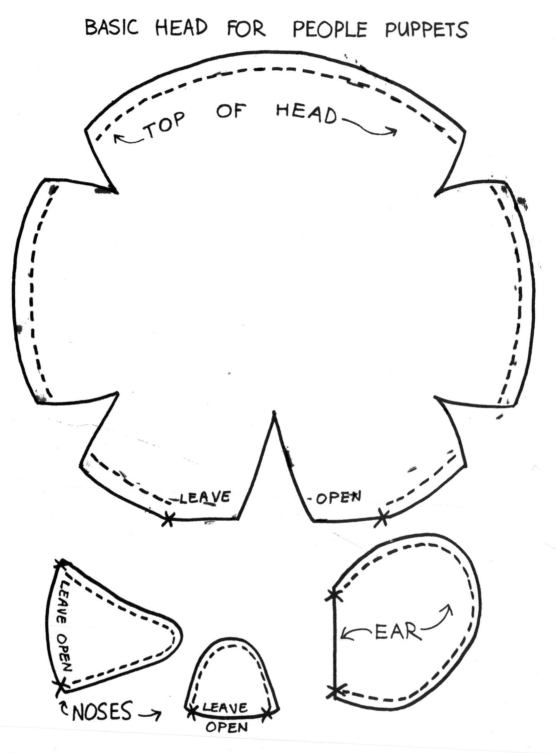

TOP OF HEAD

LEAVE - OPEN

LEAVE OPEN

NOSES →

LEAVE OPEN

EAR

56

BASIC HAND PUPPET BODY

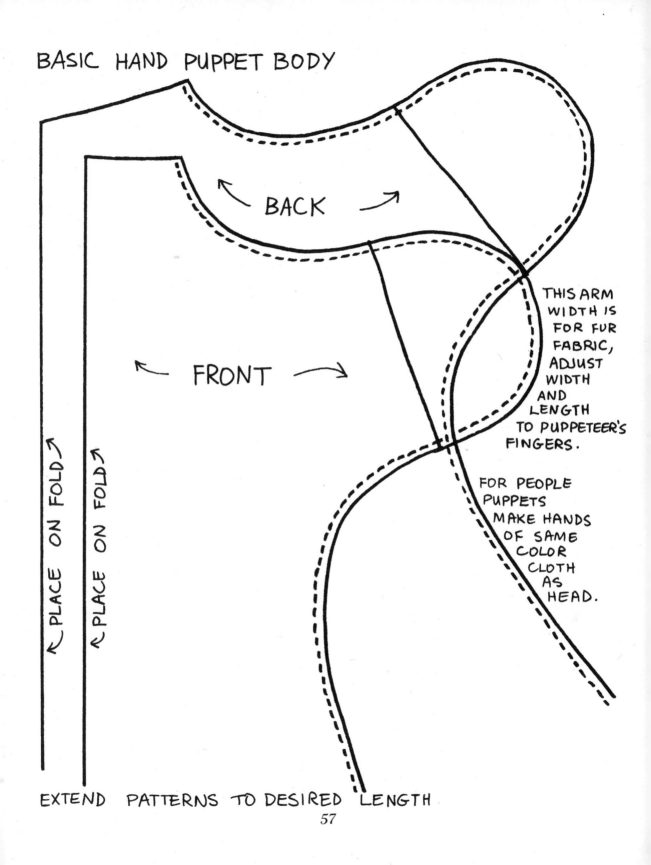

BACK

FRONT

PLACE ON FOLD

PLACE ON FOLD

THIS ARM WIDTH IS FOR FUR FABRIC, ADJUST WIDTH AND LENGTH TO PUPPETEER'S FINGERS.

FOR PEOPLE PUPPETS MAKE HANDS OF SAME COLOR CLOTH AS HEAD.

EXTEND PATTERNS TO DESIRED LENGTH

The puppeteer's fingers should reach the tips of the puppet's hands

Sew the skirt to the waist. Sew the underskirt on next. Then sew on the puppeteer's sleeve—the part of the puppet that hides the puppeteer's arm is called the sleeve. This sleeve should extend several inches below

Most skirts look best with an underskirt

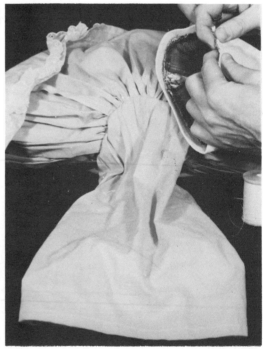

the skirt so the puppeteer's arm will never show. To me most skirts look best with an underskirt, but this is a matter of personal preference.

On a male puppet the puppeteer's sleeve usually represents trousers,

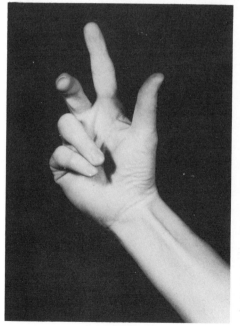

therefore it should be of a different material from the shirt. A jacket or coat may be made from the body pattern. Enlarge the jacket slightly and make the length appropriate to the character. If the shirt is to have any trimming down the front it is best to sew this on before the shirt is sewn together. All parts of the body, including hands, will look better, resist wrinkling, and last longer if lined with muslin. Make it a rule to use lining anywhere the puppeteer's hand or arm will touch.

The puppet body should fit the puppeteer's hand comfortably with room to work the puppet's hands easily. A puppet that is too snug cannot perform very well, and this is most frustrating. On the other hand, a puppet body that is too loose can also be a problem. My earliest hand puppets were made with the fronts and backs the same size. That extra cloth always bunched up in front and looked terrible; the long arms kept sliding off my fingers; and quick changes were nearly impossible.

The Tichenor frogs have feet
for a special purpose.
See text, page 61

My patterns with smaller fronts may seem strange at first, but puppets made from them stay on the hand and present a much neater appearance. You have to tailor-make a pattern to fit your own hands. The basic pattern here may need enlarging or reducing. You will know after using it one time. *See pages 56-57.*

Many people object to the lack of legs and feet on hand puppets. I have made many with them, but have ended up removing practically all of them. My frogs keep their feet, but only because they make comic entrances with their feet in their mouths, and then let the feet flop. Feet usually just get in the puppet's way and look awkward. I say forget them— or use marionettes where legs have a purpose.

Costumes. For years I worked with marionettes and would not touch hand puppets. Hand puppets could not walk, and I could not costume them as I did marionettes (overdress them might be a more apt phrase). When television forced me into using hand puppets, I soon learned that they have many advantages. They can even be dressed elegantly. In fact, you can use stiffer materials, even heavy brocades, on them because your hand is inside making them move. You can use big hooks and eyes for unfastening their clothing easily.

There seems to be a tendency to dress princesses in pale, delicate colors. While they may look very fragile and feminine when held in your hand, on stage they are apt to appear dull and drab, or washed-out. I have discovered that audiences always show a decided preference for the girls in the cast who are dressed in clear, true colors. Audience reactions to types of clothing has been noted also. A full skirt is more appealing than a slinky or straight one. A prince is more dashing in a light-colored, short cape. Long capes are for older men, and dark ones for sinister characters. Hooded capes can be worn by anyone in a fairy tale, male or female. Fur around the hood is flattering for a girl. Felt is ideal for a hooded cape. A cape does not have to be hemmed, but for regal capes use silk velvet. It drapes beautifully, moves gracefully, and its effect is worth the effort expended in hemming it.

I use buckram or heavy felt from an old hat to stiffen large hats and pointed headdresses. Cardboard is difficult to use, and cotton stuffing overbalances the head and is most uncomfortable. Puppet heads are heavy enough; and with the addition of a huge headdress, your finger will be in agony before the show is half over. The same holds true for using crowns encrusted with weighty jewels.

Single or double hennins (the pointed, medieval headdresses that literally shout "fairy tale") are always effective. Silk handkerchiefs make good veils to hang from the hennins. The silk calls for frequent pressing, but the movement it adds to a performance is worth the trouble. The determining factor in almost everything connected with puppet shows should be: does it add to the show enough to offset the bother it causes?

Do not be afraid to use a little glitter. Rhinestones and sequins can often add just the sparkle that brings a princess to life. Nothing is so regal on a puppet as a costume trimmed in white fur-cloth, ermine-tailed with a black felt marker. Fairy-tale books from your library will offer a wealth of inspiration for costumes—for everything from peasant lads to wicked queens and bonneted bunnies.

ANIMAL PUPPETS

(See patterns, pages 70-76)

A puppeteer's best friend is a good animal puppet. This calls for fur cloth, or fake fur, as the fashion folk call it. You can use terry cloth, but your puppet is apt to end up looking like a bath mitt. Make the puppet out of ordinary cloth and there is absolutely no "touch me" texture. A furry animal shoud be furry.

Short-nap fur cloth is available in practically every fabric store. Stock up on the basic animal colors: white, brown, tan, gold, gray, and black (a small quantity). In most cases it is better to use dark gray or brown instead of black. Black loses detail unless your lighting is really good. Only black trim looks satisfactory on television. Masses of black look more like a hole than an animal. And go easy on real animal furs.

62

Upper left, Prince Canine IX; right, Leonard Lion; lower left, Mr. Raccoon; right, Cousin Walrus

Leopard and tiger, when used on small things such as hand puppets, are more camouflage than effective realism. The spots interfere with features. I ended up with a lot of ocelot fur, a bargain that could never be used. A leopard puppet was turned down for a lucrative commercial because her spots were too busy. I had to make one of yellow plush and paint in the spots with markers, so the spots were controlled, and placed exactly where they did the most good. The same thing was done with a young tiger. The felt markers really are magic—just be certain to use the permanent kind.

Don't be afraid to use a lighter or brighter shade than the real animal. My brown squirrels are gold. I have a powder blue pup and a red poodle, a bright blue lion and a rather notorious green walrus. With care you can use lots of color and not be gaudy.

Fur cloth in different textures can be employed for attractive effects, smooth fur for the head of a puppet, and fuzzy fur for his ears. My raccoon boasts five different furs on his head alone, plus two more on his ringed tail.

Experiment with the basic animal patterns (*pages 70-76*). You can adapt them for making a variety of animals. Try different ears on the dog. Add hair to some of them. Girl animals are very fetching with a few curls in matching or contrasting colors.

MOUTH PUPPETS

(See patterns, pages 73-76)

Mouth puppets are operated with the fingers in the upper jaw and the thumb in the lower jaw. Since the thumb is off center, the mouth is often worked in an unwelcome angle. To overcome this problem one must learn to compensate by pushing the thumb over to the center as far as possible and bending the hand over, forcing the forefinger down, until the mouth is level. This is best practiced in front of a mirror. Bend the wrist so the puppet's eyes will look at the audience or at the other puppet to whom it is speaking. This is not a comfortable position, but it is better than offering only a view of the puppet's chin and the roof of its mouth.

To make a mouth puppet, duplicate each piece of the pattern (except the ears) in muslin as well as fur cloth. Pin the muslin pieces on the back sides of the fur counterparts. This lining should be sewn along with, and at the same time as the fur. It will give strength and provide the extra body to make the mouth work properly.

Sew the darts and the nose first. Sew the sides to the center piece. Sew the lower jaw to the pink felt mouth. Sew the back sides of the lower jaw to the sides of the head. Then sew the upper jaw to the upper half of the pink felt mouth. All these steps will be easier if the pieces are first pinned in place.

The skull (the framework or mold which gives permanent shape to the head) should be stuffed firmly and pinned inside the head. Before sewing the skull in place try the head on your hand. The skull should rest comfortably on the back of the hand. Sew the neck (or puppeteer's sleeve) to the head, making certain to sew the linings too.

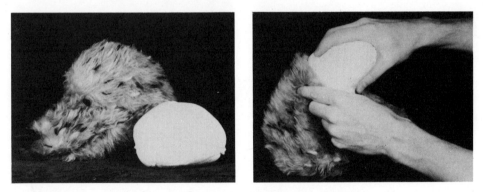

See mouth-puppet patterns, pages 73-76

Now attach the ears, but never in a straight line. Pin and then stitch them in a circular position. Long ears should be floppy. Sometimes it is necessary to sew tiny weights inside the ends of the ears to give them more "floppability."

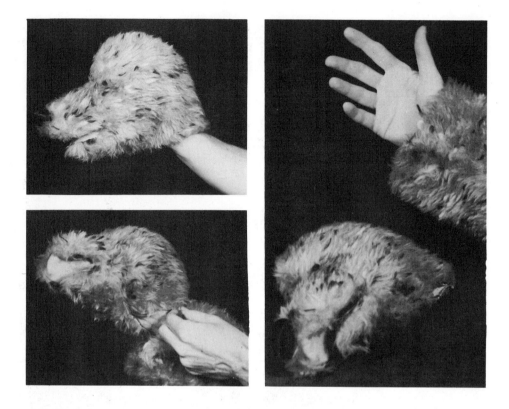

The black nose is made of an oval, cut from satin or sateen, gathered around the edge, stuffed, and caught tightly. Pin it exactly in place before sewing; it will probably need to be sewn around twice.

To keep the mouth lining (the pink felt) in place, it may be necessary to stitch a seam along the sides about three eights of an inch up, going through both the fur cloth and the pink felt. Do this on both the upper and lower jaws. This will keep the inner mouth from popping out of line. Cut a black felt oval just a bit shorter than the width of the mouth. Glue it at the very back of the mouth so that half of it is on the upper felt, and half on the lower. This should be done on all mouth puppets. It provides a rigid bar that will hold the lower jaw in place. Put the puppet on your hand to set the mouth in proper position. Remove the head most carefully and do not move it until the glue has thoroughly dried.

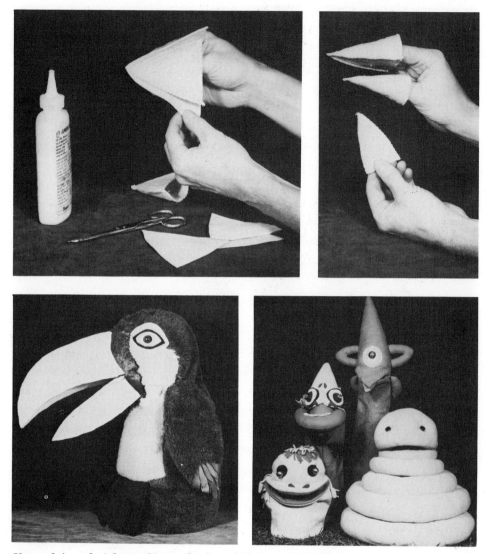

Upper left and right, making a beak or bill for a bird; lower left, a toucan rooster; lower right, various space creatures, all mouth puppets. See basic patterns, pages 73, 76

If feet are desired, sew them on three or four inches down the neck from the lower jaw. On animal mouth-puppets the paws are more practical than on a human puppet. They create the illusion that there is more to the animal than is being seen on the stage.

Once you have learned to handle this basic pattern, you can make your own patterns for other animals, varying the length of the nose, the size of the head and skull, and so on.

Fowls have smaller heads. They, too, have skulls. Their beaks or bills are made in much the same way as the mouths for the other animals, only the ends are round or pointed. Felt, in a color appropriate to the bird, should be cut and glued over the sewn mouth parts. Let the felt extend a bit beyond the edges of the mouth. Cut three upper and three lower pieces each one a fraction larger than the one to be glued under it. Glue them on, one by one, starting with the smallest. Be generous with the white glue. You are laminating the bill. After the bill dries, you may want to give it a coat of white glue to make the surface hard. For a shiny finish use two or three coats of the glue. However, most bills look best without the gloss. Like other mouth puppets, fowls should have the black piece glued in the back of the mouth. Don't forget tongues! Use red felt.

Remember that ducks and geese have rounded bills that are somewhat flat. Birds and chickens have pointed beaks that are sharper at the top. This calls for two pieces of felt at the top. You can see what I mean in the pictures of the toucan (*page 67*) and rooster puppets (*page 158*).

Bird finger puppets shown above may be made from pattern on opposite page

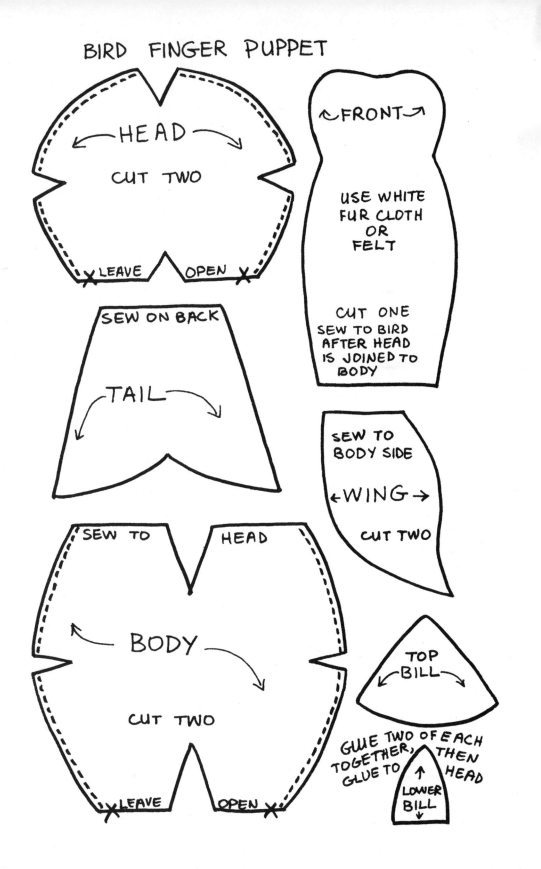

BIRD FINGER PUPPET

HEAD

CUT TWO

LEAVE   OPEN

FRONT

USE WHITE
FUR CLOTH
OR
FELT

CUT ONE
SEW TO BIRD
AFTER HEAD
IS JOINED TO
BODY

SEW ON BACK

TAIL

SEW TO
BODY SIDE

WING

CUT TWO

SEW TO   HEAD

BODY

CUT TWO

LEAVE   OPEN

TOP BILL

GLUE TWO OF EACH
TOGETHER, THEN
GLUE TO   HEAD

LOWER BILL

BASIC HEAD FOR RABBIT, SQUIRREL AND CHIPMUNK

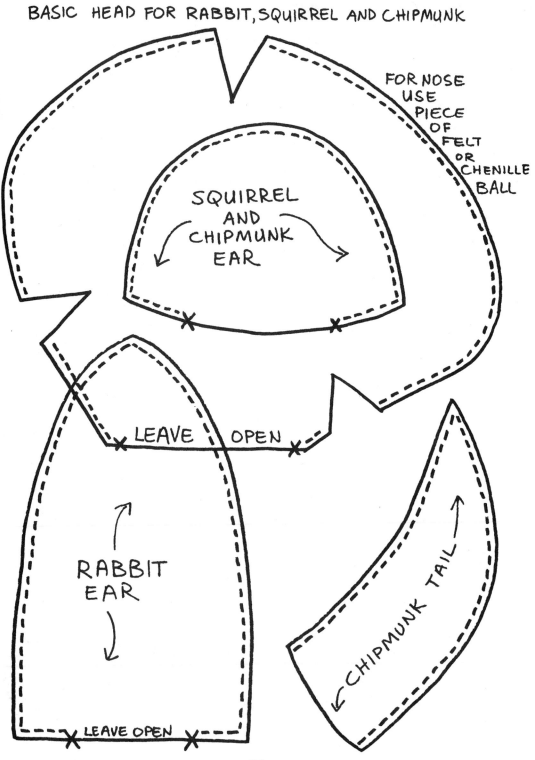

FOR NOSE
USE
PIECE
OF
FELT
OR
CHENILLE
BALL

SQUIRREL
AND
CHIPMUNK
EAR

LEAVE OPEN

RABBIT
EAR

LEAVE OPEN

CHIPMUNK TAIL

70

MOUSE HEAD

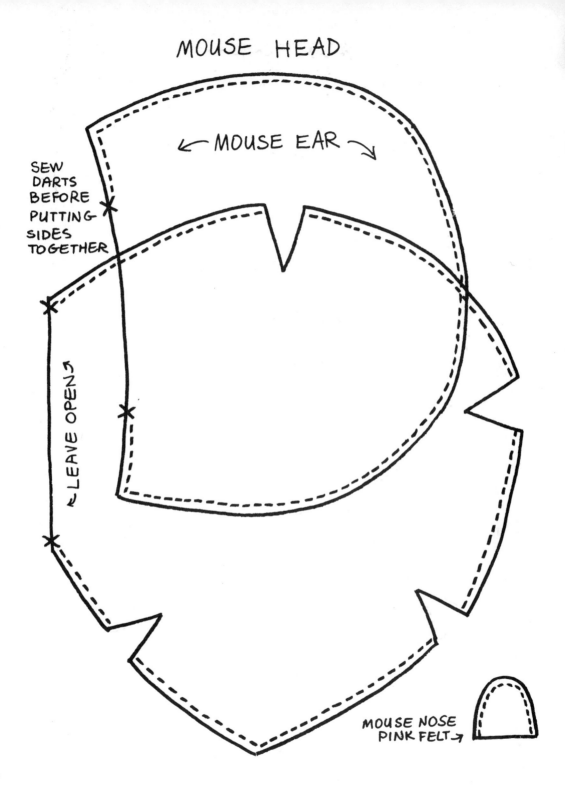

MOUSE EAR

SEW DARTS BEFORE PUTTING SIDES TOGETHER

LEAVE OPEN

MOUSE NOSE PINK FELT

71

HEAD FOR BEAR, DOG AND OTHER ANIMALS

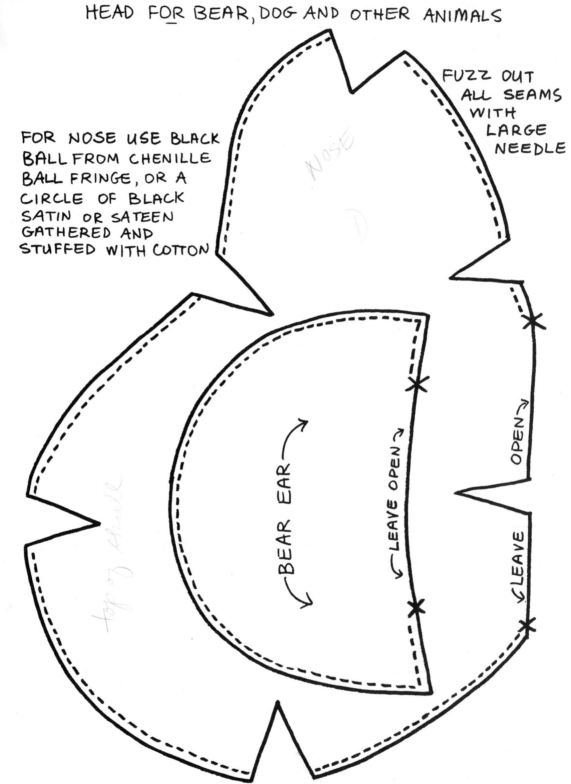

FOR NOSE USE BLACK
BALL FROM CHENILLE
BALL FRINGE, OR A
CIRCLE OF BLACK
SATIN OR SATEEN
GATHERED AND
STUFFED WITH COTTON

FUZZ OUT
ALL SEAMS
WITH
LARGE
NEEDLE

NOSE

BEAR EAR

LEAVE OPEN

LEAVE

OPEN

top of skull

72

BASIC HEAD FOR MOVING-MOUTH PUPPETS

USE AS IS FOR DOGS AND LIONS
MAKE HEAD HIGHER FOR BEARS.

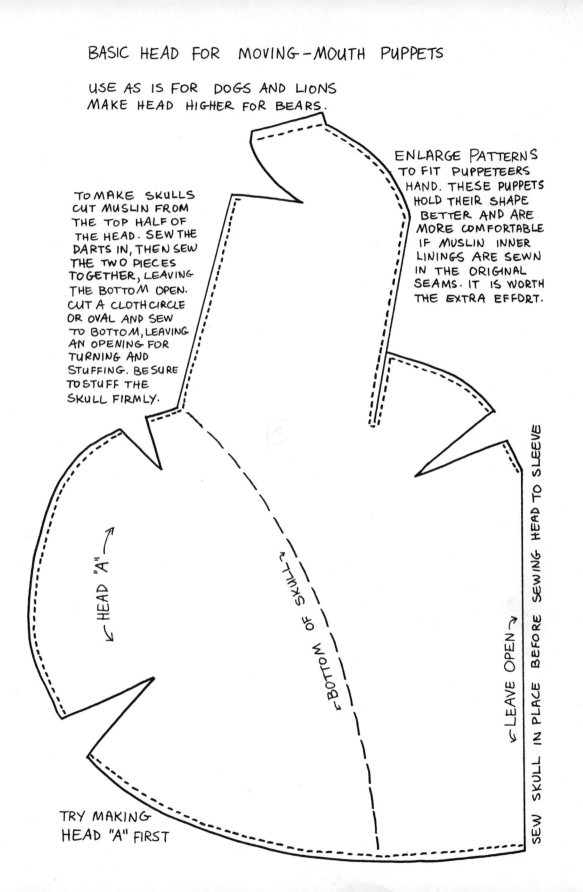

ENLARGE PATTERNS
TO FIT PUPPETEERS
HAND. THESE PUPPETS
HOLD THEIR SHAPE
BETTER AND ARE
MORE COMFORTABLE
IF MUSLIN INNER
LININGS ARE SEWN
IN THE ORIGINAL
SEAMS. IT IS WORTH
THE EXTRA EFFORT.

TO MAKE SKULLS
CUT MUSLIN FROM
THE TOP HALF OF
THE HEAD. SEW THE
DARTS IN, THEN SEW
THE TWO PIECES
TOGETHER, LEAVING
THE BOTTOM OPEN.
CUT A CLOTH CIRCLE
OR OVAL AND SEW
TO BOTTOM, LEAVING
AN OPENING FOR
TURNING AND
STUFFING. BE SURE
TO STUFF THE
SKULL FIRMLY.

← HEAD "A" →

← BOTTOM OF SKULL →

← LEAVE OPEN →

SEW SKULL IN PLACE BEFORE SEWING HEAD TO SLEEVE

TRY MAKING
HEAD "A" FIRST

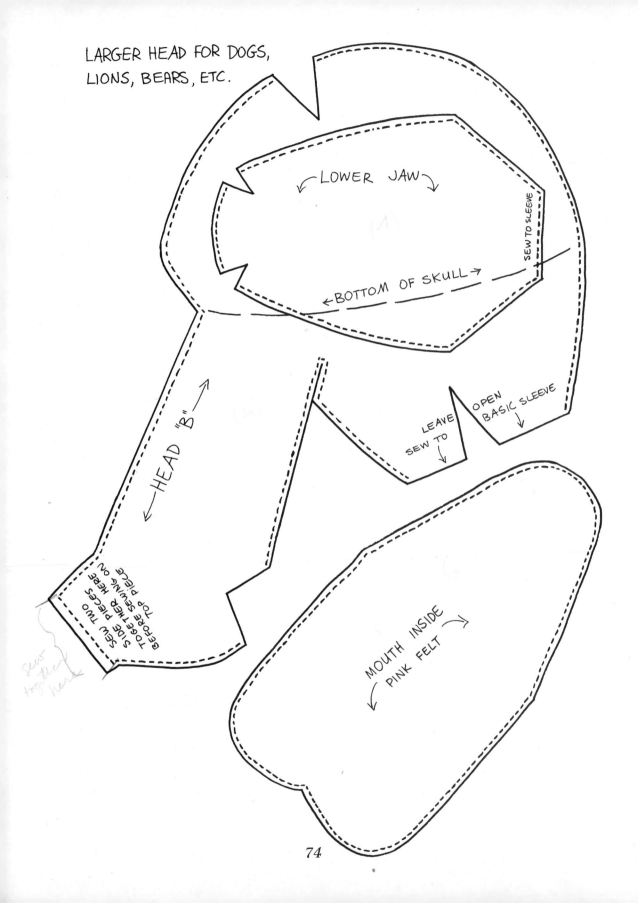

LARGER HEAD FOR DOGS,
LIONS, BEARS, ETC.

← LOWER JAW →

← BOTTOM OF SKULL →

SEW TO SLEEVE

← HEAD "B" →

SEW TWO SIDE PIECES TOGETHER HERE BEFORE SEWING ON TO PIECE

sew together here

LEAVE SEW TO

OPEN BASIC SLEEVE

MOUTH INSIDE
PINK FELT

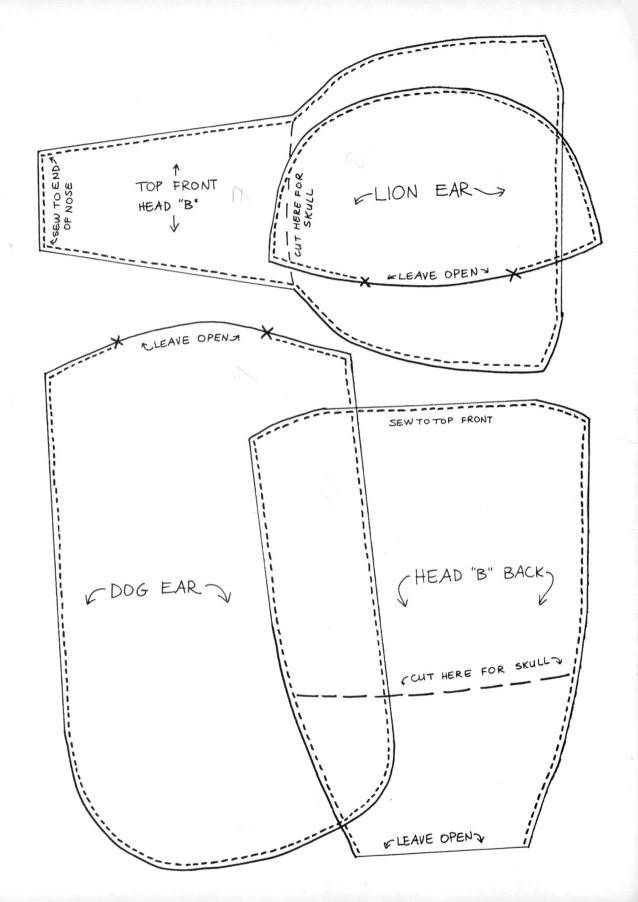

SEW TO END OF NOSE

TOP FRONT
HEAD "B"

CUT HERE FOR SKULL

←LION EAR→

←LEAVE OPEN→

←LEAVE OPEN→

SEW TO TOP FRONT

←DOG EAR→

←HEAD "B" BACK→

←CUT HERE FOR SKULL→

←LEAVE OPEN→

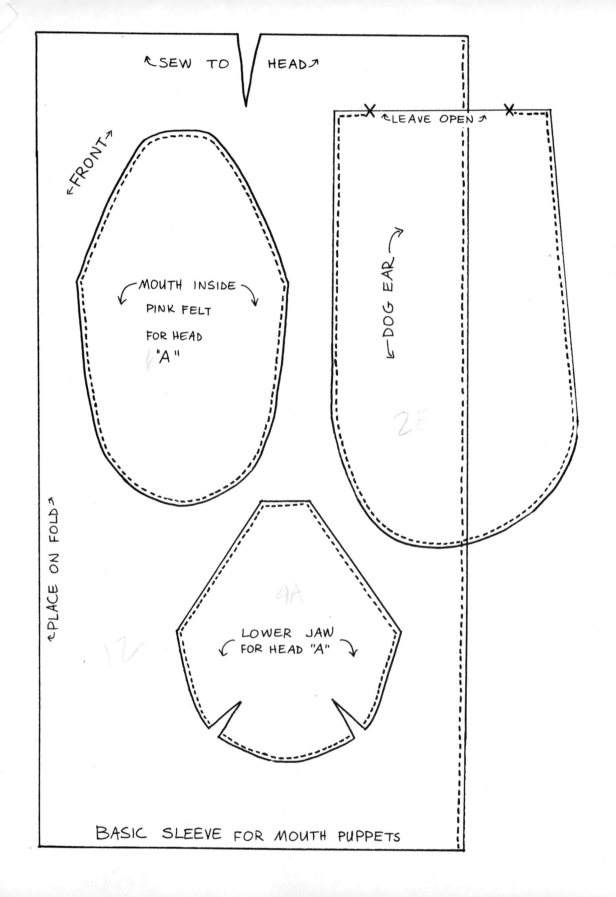

SEW TO HEAD

FRONT

LEAVE OPEN

MOUTH INSIDE
PINK FELT
FOR HEAD
"A"

DOG EAR

PLACE ON FOLD

LOWER JAW
FOR HEAD "A"

BASIC SLEEVE FOR MOUTH PUPPETS

HAND-PUPPET STAGES

There are so many books available with plans for puppet stages, big and small, simple and elaborate, that I will not go into detail on that subject. Undue stress on fancy staging is not sensible for the beginner puppeteer. Those who want stages of professional quality would do well to order plans from the Puppeteers of America. I am including pictures of stages I have used, none of them a perfect theater.

My most satisfactory dramatic productions have been done with the puppets working overhead. This method is tiring at first, but has many advantages: the puppets can pass each other, take off in flight, and move about without bumping into each other. The stage was a framework covered in front with a velvet drapery, actually a slightly damaged casket lining from a salvage store. At the top of the stage was an eight-inch board with slots cut in it at intervals so the scenery could be put in place. The scenery was attached to sticks with braces on front and back worked into the design. The scenery, which was changed frequently during the course of the play, could be put up and taken down without any hands showing. This meant that there were no curtains to be pulled for scene-changing and there was no waiting; the action was continuous. *Christmas at Creepy Castle* and *Jack and the Beanstalk* were given on this stage with great effectiveness.

My most recent hand-puppet stage has a proscenium low enough for me to sit behind a sheer scrim curtain. I can see the puppets but I am not really visible to my audience while working. And when that part of the show is over, the stage curtains can be closed, the scrim taken away, and a play presented overhead, making this a smaller version of the stage described in the preceding paragraph. It has a board with the slots, and the scenery from the big stage can be used on it.

Hand puppets can perform with much less folderol than marionettes. Some of my most-treasured moments have happened in a classroom at a desk, where the children saw me as well as my puppet Marco Polo Bear. The children never even looked at me. Marco would visit the class and answer the most remarkable questions such as "Who built the first pyramid?" Who, indeed? Marco scratched his head and thought, and then retorted, "The Egyptian slaves, of course." Luckily he thought faster than I did. It is not where you perform, but what you do, that counts.

If your puppeteers are all very near the same height, I would suggest your using as a stage the overhead board with cloth in front. With this simple setup you can use the existing stage lighting in most auditoriums. Or you can set the stage up in a doorway at home, or even in the corner of a room. Later on you can move into more elaborate stages.

Tom Tichenor arranges draperies and, in lower photographs on opposite page, works with the puppets overhead. See also page 80

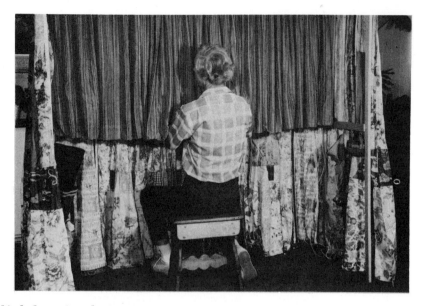

Seated behind the scrim, the puppeteer creates a moment of magic for his audience

HAND-PUPPET PLAYS

SELECTING A PLAY. The selection of a play should be governed by several practical considerations. First, how many puppeteers are available? The average stage will not hold a cast of thousands, so forget the exodus· from Egypt and forget stampedes. Do not attempt *The Golden Goose*—a thoroughly delightful story—unless you have enough hands for Dumling, three girls, the parson, the sexton, two peasants, the king, and his weepy daughter, all of whom appear at the same time. Stories with large casts are possible only when not many characters are onstage at *one* time.

Second, for whom is this production intended? Obviously, you would not plan the same program for preschoolers and high school students. There are many stories with versions that can please all ages at the same time. The secret is in your approach. If the script is genuinely funny, both children and their fathers will be amused.

Third, can the play be given without an abundance of elaborate scenery? Personally I like great castles on high mountains, ballrooms with crystal chandeliers, and stately stairways. But most of the time I have to settle for a suggestion of such grandeur on a small knoll.

With all these things to consider, what would you like to do? How about an old favorite with a new beginning? I mean *Jack and the Beanstalk*. When this version was presented, the fathers in the audience laughed hardest of all. The first half of the story is mostly original, the rest is the familiar, exciting story that children revel in.

The puppet cast can be managed by four puppeteers, or possibly in a pinch by three. Or you can have a puppeteer for each character. The more people backstage, the more confusion, so keep anyone not onstage out of the way.

My version, which begins before Jack's father was even married, was performed by animals. I used mice for Jack's family: the ugly duckling Duckie as the Beautiful Good Fairy; a fox for the man with the beans; and a rat for the giant's wife, although the giant himself is human. You can easily use all people puppets instead of animals—

simply change the animal names to people names. Nothing in the script will make the change difficult.

Since the action covers a considerable period of time, I have used a narrator to hold the story together. If you prefer a shorter play, you can cut this one in half, using only the traditional story beginning where Jack is sent to sell the cow.

Now read the play, and then we will plan the production—scenery, props, rehearsal, special effects—but, first, *read the play*.

JACK AND THE BEANSTALK

Characters

GODFREY, a penniless, young man who starts out nicely but becomes greedy. At first, the mouse wears no clothing at all; later, he dons a velvet jacket with fancy trimming

MISS MEADOW MOUSE, a very plump mouse, well-dressed and with a superior manner

FELICIA FIELDMOUSE, two puppets will be needed: one should be young and prettily dressed; the other, older and dressed in worn and tattered clothes

BEAUTIFUL GOOD FAIRY, a duck, dressed very glamorously with lots of sparkle and glitter. Must have a drab cloak that completely envelops her, and which can be easily shed onstage.

HEN That LAYS GOLDEN EGGS, a traditional little hen, who clucks and cackles and speaks in a cackly voice.

JACK, a mouse. As a baby, he is chubby and furry with pink feet and a long, gray tail. As a boy he is alert and bright and somewhat smaller than his mother.

BUTTERBALL THE COW, an ordinary cow. A mouth puppet could be used showing only the head. I prefer a cow with a body; mine was worked with two sticks inside.

SWINDLER Q. FOX, a wily gentleman with sly eyes and a sinister manner of speaking that makes each statement seem a confidential, illicit secret.

GIANT'S WIFE, a nervous rat brightly dressed with an apron and a ruffled mobcap.

GIANT, a huge human head, with black hair and beard, on a long sleeve. His cape should be very full and long, open in the front so a human hand can reach out for the egg. The large, styrofoam-ball head described in the marionette section would work well for him.

NARRATOR, only his voice is heard. A puppet narrator could appear at the side of the stage.

SCENE. The stage is bare except for a hollow tree stump on one side.

NARRATOR. Once upon a time in Merry Olde England, when such things still could happen, there lived a poor-but-honest young man called Godfrey.

GODFREY. What a beautiful day. What a beautiful day for getting married! If only I had someone to marry. (*Looks to his left.*) Why, there is the most beautiful mouse in this part of the country. Hello, Miss Meadow Mouse.

MISS M. M. Hello, Godfrey.

GODFREY. Isn't it a lovely day to get married?

MISS M. M. It certainly is a lovely day.

GODFREY. Then you'll marry me!

MISS M. M. Marry you? Why, I didn't say that.

GODFREY. But you agreed when I said it was a lovely day to get married.

MISS M.M. Oh, you silly mouse, how could I ever marry you? Are you a mouse of means?

GODFREY. I mean well.

Miss M. M. That's not what I mean. Have you any money? Do you have a bit of cheese tucked away for a rainy day?

Godfrey. Well, no, I haven't.

Miss M. M. And you expect me to marry you? Oh, I've never heard anything so funny. (*Giggles.*)

Godfrey. I didn't think it was such a funny question.

Miss M. M. Oh, you poor mouse. (*Giggles harder than ever.*) Marry you, oh, how ridiculous. (*Exits laughing.*)

Godfrey (*sadly*). I was very serious. Oh, hello, Felicia Fieldmouse.

Felicia (*entering*). Godfrey, you look so unhappy.

Godfrey. Miss Meadow Mouse laughed when I said it was a lovely day to get married.

Felica. It is a pretty day.

Godfrey. Then you will marry me!

Felicia. Not so fast! You haven't any nest egg. You haven't made your fortune.

Godfrey. Oh, I'll make my fortune someday.

Felicia. I'm very fond of you, dear, but I can't marry you without a place to live. Tell you what, if you make your fortune today, I will marry you. Now I have things to do. Bye! (*Pecks him on the cheek and exits.*)

Godfrey. Oh, thank you, Felicia! I'll make my fortune today, you'll see! Now which way do I go? I wonder where my fortune lies. I wonder.

Narrator. While Godfrey wondered, along came a poor old woman. She was tired and hungry.

Good Fairy. I am tired and hungry. Oh, am I ever tired and hungry.

Narrator. The poor-but-honest young man saw her.

Godfrey. Hello, tired, hungry old woman.

Good Fairy. Hello, poor-but-honest young man.

Godfrey. You look tired and hungry.

Good Fairy. I am, I am. Could you spare me a crumb of bread or a penny?

Godfrey. I would if I could, but I have no bread. Nor does a penny jingle in my pocket. I don't even have a pocket. Alas!

84

GOOD FAIRY. Alas!

GODFREY. I am going to seek my fortune. Come along with me. When I find my fortune, I will share it with you.

NARRATOR. At that moment they looked at the ground, sighing in despair. (*They sigh.*) And what did they see but—a gold coin!

GOOD FAIRY and GODFREY (*together*). A gold coin!

NARRATOR. They both jumped for it! (*They bang their heads together and say, "Ow."*) The young man helped Good Fairy to her feet.

GODFREY. I'm sorry. Are you all right?

GOOD FAIRY. I think so, but what of that gold coin?

GODFREY. I am young and strong and handsome and generous, and you are but a poor, tired, hungry old woman. You must take the money.

GOOD FAIRY. Ah, you will not regret your generosity. I am not what I seem.

GODFREY. You're not?

GOOD FAIRY. I told you I'm not.

NARRATOR. With that she threw off her ragged cloak, and she wasn't a poor, tired, hungry old woman at all. She was a Beautiful Good Fairy!

GODFREY. Why, you are a Beautiful Good Fairy!

GOOD FAIRY. Right. And you did the right thing, so you shall be rewarded.

GODFREY. Oh, I want no reward. Er, what is it?

GOOD FAIRY. Look in that hollow tree stump over there.

GODFREY. Oh, are you going to give me a golden goose?

GOOD FAIRY. No, silly, that's another story. Look!

GODFREY. (*Looks in.* HEN *pops up and startles him.*) Why, it's a hen A plain, ordinary hen.

GOOD FAIRY. This is no ordinary hen.

GODFREY. Oh, I understand. She is to be our chicken dinner. (HEN *shrieks and jumps back into the stump.*)

GOOD FAIRY. No, no. This hen lays golden eggs.

HEN (*jumping out and spreading her wings triumphantly*). Ta-da!

GODFREY. Golden eggs!

GOOD FAIRY. Just say, "Lay, little hen, lay. Give me a golden egg today."

And she will. But only one egg a day. You must not overdo a good thing.

GODFREY. Oh, thank you, Good Fairy, thank you.

GOOD FAIRY. You're welcome, I'm sure.

NARRATOR. And with that the Good Fairy disappeared. (HEN *disappears into the hollow stump.*) The young man had his fortune in the form of feathers. And that's how he came by the Hen That Lays Golden Eggs. He rushed back to see Felicia Fieldmouse.

GODFREY. Felicia! We can be married right away. (FELICIA *runs out.*)

FELICIA. You've made your fortune? Where?

GODFREY. There! (*Points to hen.*)

FELICIA. A hen! You must be joking.

GODFREY. She lays golden eggs. I'll show you. "Lay, little hen, lay. Give me a golden egg today." (HEN *settles down and cackles, signaling the appearance of a shiny, golden egg.*) See, our nest egg.

FELICIA. But where shall we live?

GODFREY. With this gold I will buy a pretty little cottage where our dreams can all come true.

FELICIA. Oh, Godfrey, you are a mouse among mice. And what's more, you're nice. We shall be married at once.

GODFREY. Henny, would you be our flower girl? (HEN *gladly agrees; the three exit together.*)

NARRATOR. Godfrey bought a little farm with a pretty little cottage (*Cottage appears.*) and soon the wedding party returned. (HEN *enters strewing rose petals from her basket. The bride and groom walk behind her.*)

GODFREY. It was a nice wedding—very short. There's our new home.

FELICIA. How pretty it is! You are going to follow custom and carry me over the threshold.

GODFREY. I don't feel very strong. I haven't had a bite to eat all day. (*Picks her up as though she were a watermelon.*)

FELICIA. Somehow I don't think this is quite the way it's done.

GODFREY. Oh, oh. (*He takes a step or two and drops her. She groans.*) I'm sorry. (*Helps her up.*)

FELICIA. Well, somebody has to carry someone across the threshold. Here! (*Throws him over her shoulder and trudges off with him into the cottage.*)

NARRATOR. Godfrey and Felicia were very happy in their little cottage. And their happiness was even greater when a baby boy was born: Baby Jack.

GODFREY (*Coming out of the house holding the baby, followed by* FELICIA.). Ah, such a handsome little boy. He looks just like me.

FELICIA. How true. We are so happy here in our little house with our little Jack. He is a handsome baby.

GODFREY. He is also, er, you had better take him. (*Hands baby to her.*)

FELICIA. Come to mother.

GODFREY. I've been thinking about the way we live.

FELICIA. It's perfect, isn't it?

GODFREY. For you, perhaps. But not for me.

FELICIA. What do you mean, dear, sweet husband?

GODFREY. This house! We're rich, we should live in a better house.

FELICIA. But I love our little house.

GODFREY. That's just it—it's a **little** house. I want a big house. And I want it built over there where that stump is.

FELICIA. If that's what you want, dear—(*Goes inside.*)

GODFREY. I shall have it. At once! (*Goes inside.*)

NARRATOR. So the stump disappeared (*Stump disappears.*) and a magnificent country house appeared in its place. (*Elegant house appears.*)

GODFREY (*looking out window*). It's completed. Felicia, we must move in the new house. (GODFREY *and* FELICIA *come out of cottage.*)

FELICIA. It's so big!

GODFREY. It's as big as a castle. I'll have a special room just for my golden eggs.

FELICIA. Baby Jack, see your new home? Oh, Godfrey, I hope now you will be happy. (*They go inside.*)

NARRATOR. For a while things went along nicely. Godfrey counted his gold—

GODFREY (*at upstairs window*). Three hundred and fifty eggs, three hundred and fifty-one eggs—I think I will buy that big farm over there.

FELICIA (*coming out*). But, Godfrey, you already own more land than you need.

GODFREY (*coming out behind* FELICIA). Who said anything about needing it? I just want it. I think I'll buy the Duke's castle.

FELICIA. Why?

GODFREY. So I can tear it down. It spoils my view of the river. Ha, ha. I love being rich.

FELICIA. Godfrey, I don't know what has come over you. (*Goes inside.*)

GODFREY. I'm rich, I'm rich! No one is richer than I. (*Goes inside.* MISS MEADOW MOUSE *comes up to the big house, looks at it, and shakes her head in regret.*)

MISS M. M. Ah, just think if I had married Godfrey, I would be living in that house.

GODFREY (*sticking his head out*). Eat your heart out! (*Pulls his head back inside.*)

MISS M. M. Ohhhh! (*Breaking into sobs she exits.*)

GODFREY (*coming out*). Hummm, she has a nice farm. I think I'll buy it and throw her out in the cold. Ah, but the weather is warm. I'll wait till winter, and then throw her out! Ha, ha—(*Goes back inside.*)

NARRATOR. Sometimes too much money can make a person change.

FELICIA (*coming out holding the baby*). My dear, sweet husband isn't dear and sweet anymore. He is growing greedy and selfish, I fear.

GODFREY (*coming out*). I think I will buy the king's throne. I think I'll buy his crown. Then I'll buy the palace and kick the king out!

FELICIA. No, no, Godfrey, you're going too far.

GODFREY. I'll buy anything I like and kick out anybody I don't like!

FELICIA. But you don't like anyone anymore.

GODFREY. I think you're right.

FELICIA. You don't even like your own baby son.

GODFREY. He's a rich, spoiled brat. Who could like him?

FELICIA. I like him. And I don't think you even like me.

GODFREY. How did you know? Go away, you bother me.

FELICIA. I will, I will. And I'll take the rich, spoiled brat—I mean our dear baby son—I'll take him with me.

GODFREY. Then go! Hmmm, I need a new velvet coat.

FELICIA. Goodbye, Godfrey. Jack and I will return when you have changed your mean, greedy ways. (*Exits.*)

GODFREY. I'll never change! I like myself the way I am. Rich, rich, RICH! (*Goes inside.*) Hmmm, I think I'll buy the king and make him my stableboy. Ha ha, rich, rich, RICH!

NARRATOR. As you can see, Godfrey was becoming more and more impossible. When a person grows so greedy and selfish, something is bound to happen. That night, as Godfrey sat counting his money, it happened. What happened? No one knew for certain. There was a terrible rumbling—(*Rumbling sound made by a large piece of tin or aluminum is heard.*) and the sky grew black. (*Lights go off.*) There was a smash, a crash (*Take down the big house; put up the rubble—a jumble of card-*

board and felt pieces.) and when daylight came there was no more magnificent country house, only a pile of rubble. The faithful wife decided to
return.

FELICIA (*appearing on far side of stage with Baby Jack*). Jack, we will
give him another chance. After all, he's your father, and he's my dear,
sweet, mean, selfish husband. (*Sees the rubble.*) Oh! Oh! What has
happened?

NARRATOR. A disaster, that's what. Anyone can see that.

FELICIA. Our home, nothing but crumbled stones and broken wood.
And my dear, sweet, mean, selfish husband, where is he?

NARRATOR. She searched through the ruins (FELICIA *calls out "Godfrey!*
Godfrey!"); then she found him. (*She shrieks.*) That is, what was left
of him—(FELICIA *says, "Horrors!"*) a few smashed bones and his locket
with his own picture in it that he always wore next to his heart.

FELICIA. His locket. Oh, little locket, I will keep you forever—to
remember him by. I will never part with you. (*Puts locket down.*)

NARRATOR. But the faithful wife was also a practical woman. What
about the Hen That Lays Golden Eggs?

FELICIA. I must find the hen. Without her we are poor, poor, poor!
Henny! Henny! Where are you? Come to mother.

NARRATOR. She searched in vain. The hen was not to be found.

FELICIA. Oh, dear. My son and I, what will we be now?

NARRATOR. You'll be poor, that's what!

FELICIA. But we have grown accustomed to riches, and a fine house.
Where will we live?

NARRATOR. The little cottage, where you once were so happy.

FELICIA. Yes, we will live there. Come Jack. (*She carries the baby to
the cottage and puts him inside. The rubble disappears. She comes out.*)
It's not much, but it is a roof over our heads. We'll need food. What
will I do for money? I'll have to sell something. The locket, that's what
I'll sell. (*She gets the locket and takes it inside the cottage.*)

NARRATOR. So she sold the locket with her husband's picture in it—
the one he always wore next to his heart. She sold everything they owned,
piece by piece, as the years went by. They became poorer and poorer.

90

FELICIA (*coming out, looking older, her dress plain and patched*). It wasn't like this when we had that wonderful hen. Oh, where is that lazy boy? Jack! Jack! Where are you?

JACK (*coming out, yawning*). I was taking a nap. I'm tired.

FELICIA. You're lazy, that's what you are. Why can't you go out and be nice to a good fairy or something?

JACK. I've never seen a good fairy. Things like that don't happen anymore. Nothing ever happens. Life is very dull. There's never anything to do.

FELICIA. I'll give you something to do. You're going to market.

JACK. What for? We haven't any money to buy anything.

FELICIA. You are going to sell the only thing we have left—the cow.

JACK. Sell Butterball? Oh, no, Mother, I couldn't sell her.

91

FELICIA. She's the only thing we have that's worth anything.

JACK. Who would want her? She doesn't give much milk.

FELICIA. The butcher will pay something for her. And her hide is worth a bit.

JACK. Please, Mother, don't make me sell Butterball.

FELICIA. I'm sorry, Jack, but unless we get some money we'll starve. Now, take the cow to market, and don't take one penny less than ten florins.

JACK. But, Mother—

FELICIA. No buts about it. There's a good boy. (*Goes inside.*) Make a good bargain.

JACK. Butterball! (*Cow appears.*) I can't tell her what's going to happen. Butterball, we're going for a walk. That's right.

Fox (*appearing with a basket*). What do I see? Hmmm, a suede jacket, a dozen wallets, a belt, or two or three—ah, good day, my boy. Permit me to introduce myself. I am Swindler Q. Fox.

JACK. Good day, sir.

Fox. Fine-looking bag of bones you have there.

JACK. This is Butterball, my best friend.

Fox. And where are you going?

JACK. I'm taking her to market—(*softly*) to sell her.

Fox (*with great excitement*). Sell her!

JACK. Not so loud! She doesn't know it.

Fox. Sorry. My boy, how much are you asking for her?

JACK. Not a penny less than ten florins.

Fox. Ten florins. What luck for you that I happened along. I have something in this basket worth more than ten florins.

JACK. Really?

Fox. Take a look.

JACK. All I see are beans.

Fox. Yes, but these are not ordinary beans. Not at all. These are magic beans!

JACK. Magic beans? How wonderful!

Fox. And I will give them to you for your cow there.

92

JACK. Mother wants me to make a good bargain. It's not every day that one has a chance to get magic beans!

Fox. Here are your beans. Come, cow.

JACK. You will be good to her, won't you?

Fox. I shall treat her as if she were the finest suede. Ha, ha. Good day, my boy. (*Departs with cow.*)

JACK. Goodbye, Butterball, I'll miss you. And thanks for the magic beans. Oh, I can hardly wait to tell Mother. Mother!

FELICIA (*coming out of cottage*). Are you back from market so soon?

JACK. I didn't go to market, but I made a real bargain.

FELICIA. I knew you could do it. Where is the money?

JACK. I traded the cow.

FELICIA. You did trade her for money—you did get money—you didn't get money!

JACK. I got something worth more than money. Look in this basket.

FELICIA. You traded the cow for beans! You, you just gave the cow away!

JACK. These are magic beans.

FELICIA. Magic beans? Who said so?

JACK. Swindler Q. Fox told me so himself.

FELICIA. You stupid boy, you've been deceived. There's no such thing as magic beans. I'll show you what I think of your bargain—there! (*Flings the basket of beans to the ground.*) Now, since there is no money for food, you'll have to go to bed hungry. Come inside! (*Pulls him in by his ear.*)

JACK. But, Mother—

FELICIA (*At the window*). I'll teach you to be so foolish! (*spanks* JACK, *he yells.*) Now go to sleep. (*Disappears from sight.*)

NARRATOR. Poor Jack. He really thought he had made a good bargain. As for the beans, were they magic? (*Music starts softly in background.*) Suddenly, something started growing outside the house. Could it be—a beanstalk. It grew and grew, such big beans. A real beanstalk! Truly the beans were magic after all. Jack could not sleep, so he slipped out of the house.

JACK (*coming out*). I didn't mean to be foolish. I thought they were magic beans. She doesn't appreciate me. I'd run away if I had any place to run. I wish she hadn't spilled them in the grass, I wanted to plant them. Maybe I can find a few of them in the grass. Beans, beans, bean— (*Runs into the beanstalk.*) stalk. Beanstalk! The beans were magic after all. This beanstalk goes all the way up to the sky! I'll just climb up and see where it goes. Say, this is fun. Up I go! (*He climbs, keeping to the back, until he is completely out of sight.*)

FELICIA (*at window*). I'm sorry I was so cross with Jack. He didn't mean to do anything wrong. I'll see if he's awake. Jack! He's not in his bed. He has slipped out. Just wait till I get my hands on that boy! (*Goes out.*) I'll teach him to make silly bargains. I'll—what's this? A beanstalk. And so big. And there's Jack—climbing up there. Jack, you come down from there this minute! Do you hear me? I'll give you such a spanking you'll never forget it. Jack, Jack, please come down. I'm sorry about spanking you. Please come back. I'll never spank you again. Oh, oh— (*Goes into the house crying. The house is taken off, the beanstalk slowly comes down, and the* GIANT's *castle appears.*)

NARRATOR. But Jack climbed on and on, up the beanstalk, far into the clouds, until he came to the top. (JACK *appears.*) He looked around, it was a very strange place, very bleak and barren. There was a castle, all gray and huge. He went slowly toward it, and was met by a strange woman. (GIANT's WIFE *comes out.*)

94

WIFE. What do you want, boy?

JACK. Oh, nothing, I was just looking round.

WIFE. You shouldn't be here. It's dangerous.

JACK. Why?

WIFE. Don't you know whose home this is?

JACK. No.

WIFE. It's the Giant's house!

JACK. I'm not fraid of any old giant.

WIFE. Ha! Then you haven't met him. He eats little boys like you for his supper.

JACK. Really. Who are you?

WIFE. I am the giant's wife. But I don't like him.

JACK. Why don't you run away?

WIFE. He would find me. Oh, he's a cruel man, with thieving ways. Are you hungry?

JACK. Why do you ask?

WIFE. Little boys are always hungry. I'll fix you a sandwich. Rye or whole wheat? Turkey or beef? Mustard or catchup?

JACK. A bit of everything, please.

GIANT (*offstage*). **Fee, fie, fo, fum!**

WIFE. It's the giant. We must hide you.

JACK. Where?

WIFE. In the oven there. Not a sound. Your life depends on it. (JACK *hides.*)

GIANT (*entering*). **Fee, fie, fo, fum! I smell the blood of an Englishman. Be he live or be he dead, I'll grind his bones to make my bread.**

WIFE. Hello, Giant, dear.

GIANT. **I smell fresh meat.**

WIFE. Nonsense. You only smell the roast oxen left over from yesterday.

GIANT. **I hate leftovers. I want fresh meat.**

WIFE. Calm yourself, my dear. Supper will be ready shortly. In the meanwhile why don't I fetch your hen for you? She always amuses you with her golden eggs.

95

GIANT. **Then bring her to me.**

WIFE. Your wish is my command. Come, Henny. (*Gets the hen, who comes reluctantly.*)

GIANT. **All right, Hen, lay me a golden egg.** (HEN *squawks.*) **Don't give me any of your backtalk. Lay me an egg!**

HEN. No.

GIANT. **An egg—or the axe. Wife, I'll have chicken for supper.**

HEN. No no.

GIANT. **Then get to it.** (HEN *lays a golden egg.*) **Now, another!** (HEN *protests.*)

WIFE. Now, Giant, dear, you musn't overwork the poor hen. Why don't you go wash your hands before supper.

Giant. **Why?**

Wife. Let me see your hand. It's dirty, that's why. I'll finish supper. (*Exits.*)

GIANT. **Don't be long about it. I'm hungry. I want mousemeat pie.** (*Exits.*)

JACK (*coming from behind oven*). That hen, she must the one Mother told me about. I'll take her home with me. Come, Hen, you'll like it better with us. (HEN *turns and waves as she squawks good-bye.*) Quiet. Come on! (*They run off.*) The beanstalk is over here. Hurry, Hen!

GIANT (*returning with his wife*). **I tell you, I smell fresh meat. Where is my supper?**

WIFE. Be patient. It will be ready in a moment.

GIANT. **Where is my hen? Someone has been here. Someone stole my hen. I knew I smelled fresh meat!**

WIFE. Don't upset yourself, dear Giant.

GIANT. **LOOK! Someone is running across the field. It's a—a boy! And he has my hen! I'll catch him!** (*Runs off.*)

WIFE. No, Giant, don't go. Come back! Oh, dear. (*Exits. The castle is removed, and the cottage returns to its place, along with the beanstalk.*)

NARRATOR. The Giant ran after Jack, but Jack could run faster. He climbed down the beanstalk with Hen as fast as he could. The Giant

was not far above him, but the Giant was clumsy and kept catching his toes in twisted vines.

JACK (*reaching the ground*). Mother! Mother!

FELICIA (*running out of cottage*). Jack, you're back! Oh, my boy, I'm so glad you're back. But how dare you climb up that beanstalk and cause me all that worry. You deserve a good spanking!

JACK. Later. Now I need the axe.

FELICIA. Why?

GIANT (*off stage*). **I'll catch you, you mouse!**

JACK. That's why! The axe! Hurry!

FELICIA (*fetching the axe*). Here it is! (JACK *begins to chop. The beanstalk falls.* GIANT *appears at far side of stage, as high off the ground as possible, and then falls down out of sight with a great thud [sound made by puppeteer's feet].*)

JACK. And that's the end of the Giant! Mother, look who came back with me.

FELICIA. Our hen! Our Hen That Lays Golden Eggs! We'll never be poor again. Oh, Jack, I'm so proud of you.

JACK. But what about Butterball? Home won't be the same without the cow. (*Cow moos and runs in, followed by Fox*) Butterball!

Fox. My boy, this cow is impossible. She keeps coming back this way. I've spent the entire day chasing her. This time I could not catch her.

Jack. I should like to buy her back.

Fox. But have you anything worth more than magic beans?

Jack. I will have in just a minute. Henny, would you, please? (*Hen nods "yes," runs in the house, and lays an egg. She looks out the window and asks if he wants it packaged.* Jack *nods. She comes out with the egg in a shallow basket*) A golden egg for you, Mr. Fox.

Fox. A golden egg. My boy, about that hen—would you consider—?

Jack. Never. Good-day.

Fox. Good-day. It never hurts to try. (*He starts off. The cow helps him along with her horns.*)

Jack. Now, Mother, since we shall have plenty of money, I think we should build a magnificent country house over there, and buy more land, and—

Felicia. Hold on, Jack. I think we'll do nicely in our own little cottage, just you and I and Butterball and Henny.

Jack. I suspect you're right. (*Starts looking all around.*)

Felicia. Jack, whatever are you doing?

Jack. I'm gathering a few of the beans—just in case things start getting dull around here.

Felicia. Boys will be boys.

Narrator. How true. Boys will be boys. And as long as there are fairy tales, we shall have happy endings.

(Curtain)

98

SCENERY. My scenery is made of corrugated cardboard with felt glued on. Details, lines, and shading are done with felt markers. I tacked (with glue spread on first) wooden strips on the back side with the ends sticking down at least twelve inches for handling, and for fitting into the slots on the board at the top. The slots should go halfway across the board. The sticks on the scenery should all be the same distance apart so you won't have to fumble around finding the right slots to fit. I made the error of not spacing them equally on my first scenery of this type, and castles seemed to dance a jig before settling down into the right place.

It does take quite a bit of felt for big set pieces, so you may decide to paint the cardboard instead. If so, it will look better if you glue some kind of plain cloth on first. You might try burlap or coarse sacking. Their texture is helpful, not in the painting, but in the finished appearance.

Remember to glue a strip of black felt around the edges of the cardboard so the corrugation won't show.

For some of my larger pieces, such as castles and trees, I cut two identical pieces of corrugated board and put the wooden strips between them, tacking lengths of the strips around the edges, between the cardboard, of course, to make it firm. Then I cover both sides with felt, and I have two sets in one.

To keep the scenery from toppling over backward or forward I glue small cardboard boxes to both sides of the board, cover them to match the stonework of the castle, or put a green felt bush in front of them as landscaping, or even turn them into tables or fireplaces. You will notice this in the photographs if you look carefully.

On one puppet stage I have grooves in the stage "floor." This is the stage where we stand and work with a scrim. The grooves are $\frac{1}{2}$-inch deep and the width holds scenery cut from $\frac{1}{2}$-inch plywood. This kind of scenery has to be much smaller than the set pieces used overhead.

Beware of "busy" scenery. Keep the pieces simple and clear. Use color—not harsh shades that make you blink, and that detract from the puppets, but bright, crisp tones.

For *Jack and the Beanstalk* you will need the following:

1. A hollow tree stump. I cut mine from a large oat box. It curves in almost a half circle. The roots balance it. The cardboard is covered with felt. It could be made of paper-mache.

2. Small cottage. Mine is soft yellow with a brighter thatch roof and open windows. The green shrubbery lets it stand alone.

3. A magnificent country house. Since the story is of English origin, my house is half-timbered and shingled. It, too, has open windows for the puppets to peek through.

4. Rubble. The remains of the house after it has been crushed. The different pieces have boxes in between for a dimensional effect.

5. The beanstalk. This is a long strip of green felt with leaves sewed on. The plastic beans came from a shop that sold plastic flowers. You might find them in a variety store or wholesale florist shop. I tied the beanstalk to a green cane, so it could be removed if we decided later to do *Jack* on the marionette stage.

6. The Giant's castle. This is in two sections for easier handling. One side has a high window where the hen lays her eggs, and the other side has the oven where Jack hides. Be certain that these pieces are not too large to allow room for the big giant puppet to appear between.

PROPS. Props are important to any show, and in hand-puppet shows they add much. Audiences never cease to be amused by a miniature actor actually picking up things and carrying them. However, a show that is overpropped can be a headache, mainly because of the limited space backstage. From time to time things will fall or roll off the stage. When they do, don't panic. Someone in the audience is always ready to hand it back. Just ask for it politely, say "thank you," and let the show go on.

Collecting props can turn into a real hobby. Everywhere I go I look for miniatures. I have a flax wheel from the Rhine, brassware and copperware from England, cooking pots from Denmark, and all kinds of goodies from gift shops, variety stores, and friends. Never miss an opportunity to look for something usable.

Sometimes this searching backfires or gets out of hand. Felicia Fieldmouse started collecting little plates (actually butter pats) several years ago. Gradually the collection began to encompass antiques. Now her collection is so valuable that it cannot be used onstage, and is used only for photographs and in displays. But, being devoted to the theatre, Felicia started another collection of plates—plastic and tin ones—that can be used on stage with abandon.

Wooden objects have been sanded free of the souvenir marks, had labels scraped off and painted over. The shapes and sizes are the main things.

For the stage using something a bit too big is better than using something too small. Look at a children's book. Notice that a mouse with a pitcher that is big makes a more appealing picture than a mouse with a pitcher so tiny you can hardly see it. Overscale props will make little animals seem smaller. When you have an adult hand puppet and want to make it seem larger than it is, give it a small prop.

Avoid things with really rough edges and snags. It is frustrating when a prop refuses to turn loose of a puppet's hand.

Props for our play are not difficult to come by:

1. Gold piece. Cut one from corrugated cardboard and cover with gold foil, or use a "real" gold coin from a charm bracelet or piece of jewelry. I used a gold-paper-encased piece of chocolate.
2. Gold eggs. Plastic Easter eggs sprayed gold. Keep three handy.
3. Little basket (with rose petals, perhaps), for the hen to carry as flower girl.
4. Locket. Use a real locket, or a coin that looks like one, on a bracelet chain.
5. Basket with beans. Save a bunch of beans from the stalk and fasten them in a basket for the trading scene.
6. Axe. For safety's sake use a plastic or wooden one to chop down the beanstalk.
7. Basket with gold egg, to buy back the cow. This egg should be glued or taped to the basket.

PRODUCTION. When you have made the puppets and the scenery, and assembled the props, you are ready to begin production.

In *the Rehearsal* the first thing to tackle is the blocking, that is, the traffic problem. In a puppet booth, puppets cannot pass each other: they have to enter and exit from the same side. Working overhead they can pass, and this gives you more freedom in the staging. Be consistent. If JACK goes off to play on one side, let him return on that side. It is always difficult for a playwright to give specific directions that a director will not find impossible to follow if he has only a few puppeteers to work with. But no matter what the playwright says, you will find what you can and can't do when you start running through the play.

Before real rehearsals begin I would suggest that you play with the puppets. Get to know them. Learn what they can and can't do. Each puppet has its built-in quirks: one can turn its head beautifully; another has a funny wobble. Try different voices. Have fun with them. Then when the actual rehearsal of the play begins, you will have already developed your characters. It will then be just a matter of learning lines and movements.

JACK seems such an easy part, but he is not all that easy to play. He has to be lazy and reluctant; at the same time, he has to be full of fun and appealing. He is never mean or recalcitrant. Think of him as adventuresome and happy-go-lucky.

MOTHER starts out as a pleasant lady, but circumstances wear her down. Even so, she is never ugly, or overly harsh.

GODFREY is a fun part. He starts out as an innocent man, open and generous. Easy money doesn't turn him into a playboy; it makes a greedy man of him. He develops a mean streak. This is necessary so we don't mind when he gets crunched. On the other hand, he plays his meanness for laughs, so the disaster does not make anyone cry—not even his widow.

THE BEAUTIFUL GOOD FAIRY was played by Duckie in our production, and she is noted for brief deliveries in her "quacky" voice. The part was tailored for her. You may use any kind of creature you choose, but let her be crisp in her retorts.

I am personally given to much ad-libbing during a performance. Some-times this can be an asset to a show—but only if the remarks are in keeping with the character who says them. It isn't cricket to get a laugh at the the expense of the play. Above all else, be prepared for your first performance.

The Performance should, if humanly possible, start on time. Nothing sours anticipation more than a long wait.

Use recorded music only when it has a definite purpose. Dialogue is difficult to understand when music is too loud or distracting.

Check out your sound system before the audience comes in. One of my pet peeves is having people backstage playing around with the microphones while the audience is coming in or waiting. When the microphones are on, nothing should be said or done that will be broadcast. Snickers and giggles are definitely unprofessional.

Have the puppets, props, and scenery organized so that each thing can be reached when it is needed.

Listen to your audience. Play to them. You cannot act in a vacuum. You must relate to your audience, and your puppets must relate to each other. Listen. Pay attention. Leave your daydreaming for another time. Keep the play moving. Act with your hands, naturally, but also act with your voice, your mind, and your heart. If you care and love—and can project this through your puppet—you have a show!

The Critique comes after the performance. Whether it is the first or the last performance, have a brief discussion, if time permits, of what was right and what was wrong with the show. You can do it a day later, but it will not be as effective without the immediacy of the moment right after the curtain closes. The one in charge should make a few notes of things to be repaired, stage business that needs to be changed, improved, or thrown out, or what should be done to make a certain scene play better. Then the group should consider what the audience reacted to most. It is never too late to try for improvement. And don't forget to give a few roses and pats on the back. For as in sports puppeteering depends on teamwork.

WHY THE BEAR HAS A STUMPY TAIL
(A new version of a Norse folktale)

Characters

MRS. RABBIT, a nice housewife rabbit

LITTLE RED RIDING RABBIT, Mrs. Rabbit's daughter (you might prefer to call her Rosamund or Ruth)

PROFESSOR GROUNDHOG, a nice, scholarly, old gentleman

BLOSSOM POSSUM, a rather fluttery lady

CECIL BEAR, a vain, self-centered bear with a long, bushy, removable tail.

MR. FOX, a very clever fellow indeed

(Other animal puppets may be substituted for these characters, excepting the bear and the fox. They are the only ones in the original tale.)

Props

Basket of honey buns

Tea service with tray

String of fish

Act I

SCENE. *Mrs. Rabbit's parlor, a comfortable, middle-class room, with some chairs and a table set for a tea party.* MRS. RABBIT *is onstage.*

MRS. RABBIT. Oh, I want everything to be perfect. This must be the nicest tea party ever given in this forest. Oh, where is that child with the honey buns?

LITTLE RED RIDING RABBIT (*entering*). Mommy!

MRS. RABBIT. Oh, Little Red Riding Rabbit, I'm so glad you're back. Did you get the honey buns?

LITTLE RED RIDING RABBIT. Yes, and Mr. Squirrel said to tell you—

MRS. RABBIT (*interrupting*). Never mind that. Let me have the honey buns, sweet.

LITTLE RED RABBIT. But, Mommy, Mr. Squirrel said—

MRS. RABBIT. Now now, dear. Oh, what lovely honey buns. Mr. Squirrel always has the tastiest and prettiest pastries in his shop.

LITTLE RED RIDING RABBIT. He told me to be sure and tell you—

MRS. RABBIT. Little Red Riding Rabbit, I told you I can't listen now. My guests will be here any moment. You run outside and play.

LITTLE RED RIDING RABBIT. May I stay inside for the tea party?

MRS. RABBIT. This party isn't for little bunnies. It's for important people. Professor Groundhog is coming, Blossom Possum will be here, and most important of all, Cecil Bear will be here. Now, run along.

LITTLE RED RIDING RABBIT. I wish you'd let me tell you—

MRS. RABBIT. Later dear, later. (*Pushes* LITTLE RED RIDING RABBIT *out.*) Now, to put the buns on the tea table.

(*A knock on the door is heard.*)

MRS. RABBIT. Oh, dear, a guest. I do hope it isn't Cecil Bear. I'm not ready. Come in.

PROFESSOR GROUNDHOG (*entering*). Is this the right house?

MRS. RABBIT. Oh, Prof. Groundhog, do come in.

PROFESSOR GROUNDHOG. You're sure this is the right house?

MRS. RABBIT. Of course. I'm Mrs. Rabbit, and this is where you're coming to tea.

PROFESSOR GROUNDHOG. Yes, yes.

MRS. RABBIT. Come right over here and make yourself at home.

BLOSSOM POSSUM (*entering*). Yoo-hoo, anyone home?

MRS. RABBIT. Blossom Possum, do come in.

BLOSSOM POSSUM. I do hope I'm not late.

MRS. RABBIT. Oh, no. You're a little early.

PROFESSOR GROUNDHOG. Why, hello, Mrs. Squirrel, how are you?

BLOSSOM POSSUM. I'm not Mrs. Squirrel.

PROFESSOR GROUNDHOG. Yes, yes, I can see that you're not. Hmmmmm, you're Mona Lizard, yes yes.

BLOSSUM POSSUM. No, no. I'm Blossom Possum.

PROFESSOR GROUNDHOG. Oh, of course you are. Yes, yes, I'm getting so absentminded.

BLOSSOM POSSUM. Yes, yes—I mean, you certainly are. Oh, Ruby Rabbit, can I do anything to help?

MRS. RABBIT. I don't think so, thank you, Blossom. I do hope everything goes well. Cecil Bear is coming.

BLOSSOM POSSUM. Oh, how exciting. He has the biggest, bushiest tail in all the forest.

PROFESSOR GROUNDHOG. Yes, yes, but he's always bragging about it.

MRS. RABBIT. I have the kettle on so we can have hot tea; and aren't these the loveliest honey buns you have ever seen!

PROFESSOR GROUNDHOG. Ooohhh—

BLOSSOM POSSUM. Yes, Yes.

MRS. RABBIT. Mustn't touch.

CECIL BEAR (*entering, announcing himself vibrantly*). Here I am.

ALL. Oh, Cecil Bear!

CECIL BEAR. Now the party can start. The most important bear in the world is here.

MRS. RABBIT. Do come in and make yourself at home, Cecil.

CECIL BEAR. You may call me Lord Bruin.

ALL. Lord Bruin!

CECIL BEAR. I decided to give myself a title. After all, I have the biggest, bushiest, most decidedly magnificent tail in the forest.

BLOSSOM POSSUM. Indeed it is.

MRS. RABBIT. If you will excuse me a moment, I'll see if the teakettle is boiling. (*Exits.*)

CECIL BEAR. Well, Blossom Possum, don't you wish you had a bushy tail like mine?

BLOSSOM POSSUM. Oh, that would be nice, I suppose, but my tail does nicely hanging upside down on a tree, the way possums do.

CECIL BEAR. Silly possums.

BLOSSOM POSSUM. I beg your pardon.

CECIL BEAR. Stupid possums, you should have bushy tails. If I were you, I'd hide in shame.

BLOSSOM POSSUM. Oh, what a dreadful bear you are. I don't care if Ruby Rabbit is one of my best friends, I'm not going to stay here

and be insulted by a bear. Good-bye, Professor Groundhog. Tell Ruby I couldn't stay. (*Runs off.*)

PROFESSOR GROUNDHOG. Yes, yes. I mean, wait, wait.

CECIL BEAR. Oh, let her go. That will mean more refreshments for me. Ummm, what have we here? Honey buns! I love honey buns.

PROFESSOR GROUNDHOG. Yes, yes.

CECIL BEAR. I love anything with honey in it. (*Gobble, gobble*) Delicious.

PROFESSOR GROUNDHOG. Really, Cecil, you shouldn't eat up all the buns.

CECIL BEAR. I'll do as I please because I have such a big bushy, beautiful tail. (*Gobble*)

PROFESSOR GROUNDHOG. Such manners.

CECIL BEAR. Oh, keep your opinions to yourself, you stupid old professor.

PROFESSOR GROUNDHOG. Well, I have never in all my groundhog days been spoken to in such a manner.

CECIL BEAR. Why don't you go home? Nobody needs you here.

PROFESSOR GROUNDHOG. I think I will, yes, yes. I've never known such arrogance and rudeness. (*Exits.*)

CECIL BEAR. Wish I had some more buns. Mrs. Rabbit! I want more buns.

MRS. RABBIT. (*Enters with teapot.*) Oh, there are plenty of buns on the table.

CECIL BEAR. Not anymore.

MRS. RABBIT. What? The buns are gone! And where are the other guests?

CECIL BEAR. They left.

MRS. RABBIT. They left! But why?

CECIL BEAR. They bothered me, so I told them to leave.

MRS. RABBIT. But you can't tell them to leave. This is **my** house.

CECIL BEAR. Well, I did. And I ate all the honey buns, and I want more.

MRS. RABBIT. There aren't anymore. That was all I had. Oh, dear, this is terrible.

CECIL BEAR. Give me some tea! I want some peppermint tea.

MRS. RABBIT. This is sassafras tea. It's very good.

CECIL BEAR. You knew I like peppermint tea best. Why didn't you make it? Oh, what a stupid hostess!

MRS. RABBIT. Oh, my tea set! You spilled the tea on my carpet, and my cups—ohhhh, Cecil Bear, will you leave? Go. At once!

CECIL BEAR. Hmmmph! No more honey buns. I'll take my big, bushy tail and go elsewhere.

MRS. RABBIT. I don't care where you go, just as long as you get out of my house and never come back. (*Shoves him out.*)

CECIL BEAR. Don't you dare touch my big, beautiful tail. You might soil the fur with your fingers. (*Leaves.*)

MRS. RABBIT. Oh (*sob*), I've never been so angry and upset.

LITTLE RED RIDING RABBIT (*running in*). Oh, the house is a mess.

Mrs. Rabbit. It's all that bear's fault.

Little Red Riding Rabbit. You should have listened to me, to what Mr. Squirrel said.

Mrs. Rabbit. And just what did Mr. Squirrel say?

Little Red Riding Rabbit. That you should never invite that bear to your home, because he'll eat you right out of it.

Mrs. Rabbit. Oh, why doesn't he hibernate like other bears.

(Curtain)

Act II

Scene. *Snowy Lakeside, a bare tree and a few rocks topped with snow.*

Mr. Fox. Ah, good-day, Blossom Possum.

Blossom Possum. Oh, is it? I hadn't noticed, Mr. Fox.

Mr. Fox. The first big snow of winter, the lake frozen over, the world a veritable fairyland of snowy white, and you didn't notice. That's not like you, Blossom.

Blossom Possum. I know. It's just that I'm upset. I ran into Cecil Bear, and he stood in my way bragging about his big bushy tail until the store closed, and I couldn't get my possum patties for dinner.

Mr. Fox. That bear. He refuses to hibernate like other bears. He wants to stay up all winter just so he can show off that long bushy tail.

Blossom Possum. One of these days I hope someone teaches him a lesson about bragging and being so rude.

Mr. Fox. Foxes are clever, you know, and should the opportunity present itself, I'll teach Cecil Bear a thing or two.

BLOSSOM POSSUM. I must be on my way now, Mr. Fox. Good-day. (*Exits.*)

MR. FOX. Good-day, Blossom Possum. Hmmmm, the lake is frozen and —what's this? A string of fish. Some fisherman must have dropped them. Too bad. Ho, ho, do I see that braggy bear coming this way? Hmmmm, with this string of fish I could teach him a lesson. I'll do it. Ah, greetings, Cecil Bear.

CECIL BEAR (*entering*). Oh, Mr. Fox, have you noticed how magnificent my tail is?

MR. FOX. And have you noticed what I have here?

CECIL BEAR. A string of fish. Nothing to compare with my—a **string of fish!**

MR. FOX. I can hardly wait to go home and fry them. Nothing like fox-fried, fresh fish on a wintry day.

CECIL BEAR. However did you catch them?

110

MR. FOX. Well, it was quite tricky. I'm sure no one else could do it.

CECIL BEAR. Tell me, how?

MR. FOX. I caught them with my tail, but you could never do it.

CECIL BEAR. I can do anything with my big, bushy tail. Just tell me how. I love fish.

MR. FOX. First, you break a hole in the ice. Then you put your tail down into the icy water. It will be cold, but that's when the fish are biting. When you can't stand it any longer, you give your tail a sharp pull to the side, and there you are, with a string of fish. Now I must be on my way. Ah, I can taste it already, delicious, fox-fried fish. Ummmm. Too bad you can't catch fish with your tail. Bye now. (*Exits.*)

CECIL BEAR. I'll show you. My tail is bigger and bushier than that fox's. He said to break a hole in the ice with a stick—I'll find a stick. Now to break the ice, so. The next part doesn't appeal to me: putting my big beautiful tail down into that cold water—but I do love fish. Here goes, YOW! It's cold. It's colder than I thought, it's awfully cold. It's bitterly co-o-ld. Oh, I can't stand it—but the thought of fresh fish, frying fragrantly. . .ooohhhh—

LITTLE RED RIDING RABBIT (*strolling in*). What are you doing, Mr. Bear?

CECIL BEAR. I'm fishing. Now run along.

LITTLE RED RIDING RABBIT. Aren't you cold?

CECIL BEAR. Yes, I am. I should think there would be enough fish caught by now. I'll pull my tail sharply to the side, like this (*Moves.*) —OWWWW! And where are my fish?

LITTLE RED RIDING RABBIT. Where is your tail?

CECIL BEAR. My tail? It's gone! It broke off—

LITTLE RED RIDING RABBIT. Oh, there it is, frozen in the ice.

CECIL BEAR. I no longer have a big, beautiful, bushy tail.

LITTLE RED RIDING RABBIT. Now you're like all the other bears.

CECIL BEAR. Oh, this is dreadful. If I'm like all the other bears, I'll have to act like other bears. No one will put up with my manner. I have nothing to show off.

LITTLE RED RIDING RABBIT. Wait till everyone sees you now.

CECIL BEAR. Oh, what shall I do? What shall—there's only one thing for me to do.

LITTLE RED RIDING RABBIT. What's that?

CECIL BEAR. Behave myself, and hibernate like the other bears. That's what I shall do. See you next spring, Bunny. (*Exits.*)

LITTLE RED RIDING RABBIT. Have a good sleep, Mr. Bear. You know what, I think he's going to be much nicer with a stumpy tail than he was when he had the biggest, bushiest tail in all the forest.

(Curtain)

CHRISTMAS AT CREEPY CASTLE

Characters

WITCHIE, two figures, one scruffy-looking, the other elegant and colorful.

BAH HUMBUG, a real bug, old with a grey beard

GHOST, has a flexible face

MRS. SANTA CLAUS, very traditional, plump and sweet

SANTA CLAUS, two figures, the first in traditional red cap and coat, the second in shirtsleeves, wearing green suspenders

OLD ELFRIEDA THE ELF, doddery and stooped, and extremely absent-minded

IRMATRUDE ELF, a pretty girl-elf

MURGATROYD ELF, a chipper boy-elf

TWO PENGUINS, you know how penguins are

DANCER REINDEER }
PRANCER REINDEER } with antlers and harness

MOTHER REINDEER, without antlers

BROOM, an extraordinary Magic Broom, belonging to Witchie. (A handle positioned below the straw part makes proper manipulation possible)

112

Props
Several stacks of letters
Letter from Witchie
Bell
Pencil or Pen
Postcard to Witchie
Several small teddy bears
Big pack filled with toys
Small pack filled with toys, with
    loop at top to fit on broomstick
Basket with lid, or box with airholes,
    with kitten inside
Long stick with hook on top for
    hanging tinsel
Silver tinsel
Wrapped package for Bah Humbug
Andirons with blazing felt fire
    and logs

Act I

SCENE. *Creepy Castle, a cold, crumbling Gothic ruin*

WITCHIE (*lurking outside*). It's Christmas time again. I can tell by the decorations and lights in the town below. Brrr. (*Shivers.*) It's cold out here. I had better go inside and get warm. (*Goes inside.*) Brrr. It's colder in here than it is outside. Creepy Castle is always dreary, but it's worse this time of year. Hark! Do I hear silent footsteps in the snow? Only one person would be out on a night like this: my gloomiest and most disagreeable dear friend. (BAH HUMBUG *comes to the side of the castle and rings the bell.*) Come in, Bah Humbug! (BAH HUMBUG *enters.*)

BAH. How did you know it was I?

WITCHIE. Who else would be out—

BAH (*finishing her sentence*). On a night like this? I knew you were going to say that, Witchie. Bah!

WITCHIE. And I knew you were going to say that. Make yourself at home.

BAH. If I wanted to be at home. I would have stayed there.

WITCHIE. Here it is the holiday season, Bah. What's Santa Claus going to bring you?

BAH. Santa Claus! There's no such person as Santa Claus.

WITCHIE. How can you say that?

BAH. Easy. There is no Santa Claus. There!

WITCHIE. There is, too. Everybody believes in Santa Claus.

BAH. I don't. Have you ever seen him?

WITCHIE. No.

BAH. Has he ever brought you anything?

WITCHIE. No.

BAH. That proves it!

WITCHIE. It doesn't prove a thing.

BAH. It does, too. If there is such a person, why hasn't he brought you a gift?

WITCHIE. Maybe it's because I haven't written to him.

BAH. Bah, humbug!

WITCHIE. I'll write him a letter. When he answers it, that will prove he exists.

BAH. He won't answer. He won't. I know he won't, because he doesn't exist.

WITCHIE. I'll show you! I'll get a pen and paper and write him this very night. Where's my paper? Where's my pen? Here we are! Now, Dear Santa—

(Curtain)

Act II

SCENE. *Santa's home at the North Pole*

MRS. SANTA (*entering, licking her fingers*). Ummmm, that chocolate candy is delicious. The best yet.

114

OLD ELFRIEDA (*backing up the pretend steps*). Mrs. Santa Claus, Mrs. Santa!

MRS. SANTA. What is it, Old Elfrieda?

OLD ELFRIEDA. Where are you, Mrs. Claus?

MRS. SANTA. I'm right here.

OLD ELFRIEDA. I hear you, but I don't see you.

MRS. SANTA. I'm right behind you.

OLD ELFRIEDA. What's that? (*Bumps into* MRS. CLAUS, *knocking her down.*) Oops! Mrs. Claus, what are you doing on the floor? Here, let me help you up.

MRS. SANTA. Thanks, Old Elfrieda. How are things in the sewing room?

OLD ELFRIEDA. Just terrible. I can't find the red doll dresses. I looked high (*Looks up.*), I looked low (*Looks down.*), I looked on the table—and under the table. (*Pantomimes.*) I looked in the drawers (*pulls out imaginary drawer, looks in, closes it.*) and on the shelves. No red doll dresses. Not anywhere.

MRS. SANTA. Did you look on the dolls that are wearing red dresses?

OLD ELFRIEDA. On the dolls? Oh, of course, that's where they are. I don't know what I'd do without you, Mrs. Claus. Well, I must get back to work.

MRS. SANTA. Be careful on the stairs; don't fall.

OLD ELFRIEDA. I never fall. Never. (*Falls.*) Oops! I fell.

MRS. SANTA. Did you hurt yourself?

OLD ELFRIEDA. Oh, no. Back to work. (*Exits.*)

MRS. SANTA. I really should see about the candy canes—

IRMATRUDE (*running in*). Mrs. Santa! Mrs. Santa! We have run out of curlers in the doll factory. How can we curl the dolls' hair?

MRS. SANTA. When I was a little girl, we didn't have curlers. We rolled our hair around a pencil and pinned the curls in place with a hairpin.

IRMATRUDE. Where will we find hairpins?

MRS. SANTA. In my dresser, the top, left-hand drawer.

IRMATRUDE. Oh, thank you, Mrs. Claus. (*Exits.*)

MRS. SANTA. I wonder if we have enough raisins for the gingerbread boys' eyes?

OLD ELFRIEDA (*backing up the steps again*). Mrs. Claus! Mrs. Santa Claus!

MRS. SANTA. What is it now?

OLD ELFRIEDA. Where are you, Mrs. Claus?

MRS. SANTA. I'm right behind you.

OLD ELFRIEDA. I hear you, but I don't see—oops! (*Knocks* MRS. CLAUS *down again.*) Mrs. Claus, what are you doing on the floor again? Here, let me help you up.

MRS. SANTA. Thank you, dear. You really should look where you're going. Another problem?

OLD ELFRIEDA. It's the blue doll dresses. I can't find the blue doll dresses anywhere. (*Pantomines the searching action again.*) I looked high, I looked low; I looked on the table, and under the table. I looked in the drawers, on the shelves. No blue doll dresses. Not anywhere.

MRS. SANTA. Did you look on the dolls wearing blue dresses?

OLD ELFRIEDA. On the dolls? Oh, of course, That's where they are. Bless you, Mrs. Claus. I'll get back to work.

MRS. SANTA. Be careful on the stairs. Don't fall.

OLD ELFRIEDA. I never fall. (*Falls.*) Oops! I fell.

MRS. SANTA. Are you all right?

OLD ELFRIEDA. Yes, indeed. Back to work. (*Exits.*)

MRS. SANTA. I really should see about the ribbons for the packages.

MURGATROYD (*running in*). Mrs. Santa Claus!

MRS. SANTA. What now, Murgatroyd?

MURGATROYD. We have run out of nails in the toy room. How can we make wooden toys without nails? I ask you, how?

MRS. SANTA. Have you tried glue? I think glue would do nicely, and we have a barrel of glue in the cellar.

MURGATROYD. Now, why didn't I think of that? Thanks, Mrs. Claus. But first I have to go to the post office. (*Goes out*)

MRS. SANTA. I wonder who will come dashing in next?

SANTA. (*dashing in, wearing his coat and hat*). Hello, Momma. I've just been to the Christmas Tree Forest. Lots of nice trees this year. Very nice Christmas trees.

Mrs. Santa. That's good, Santa. You had better go downstairs and take off your heavy clothes.

Santa. You're right. Call me when the mail comes. (*Exits.*)

Mrs. Santa. It's about time for Old Elfrieda to come up and knock me down again. This time I'll move out of her way. (*Two penguins enter and ring the bell at the far end of the house.*) Now, who can that be? (*The penguins come to Mrs. Santa.*)

Mrs. Santa. Come in.

First Penguin. Pardon me, but is this the South Pole?

Mrs. Santa. The South Pole? Oh, no. This is the North Pole. You're in Santa's workshop.

Second Penguin. The North Pole! I told you we made the wrong turn at the equator.

First Penguin. How do we get to the South Pole?

Mrs. Santa. Just start walking. Anyway you go from the North pole is south.

Second Penguin. Thank you very much. Good-bye.

Mrs. Santa. Good-bye. Do come again when you can stay longer.

First Penguin. This time I'll lead the way. Follow me. (They *leave*.)

Mrs. Santa. Never a dull moment here. I wonder what will be next?

Mrs. Deer (*from a window in the reindeer barn*). Mrs. Santa, are you home?

Mrs. Santa. Yes, I am, Mrs. Deer.

Mrs. Deer. I have a question for you. (*Comes over to* Mrs. Santa.)

Mrs. Santa. Come inside, dear.

Mrs. Deer. Oh, I do need your help. It's about my sons, Dancer and Prancer.

Mrs. Santa. I hope they're not up to some mischief.

Mrs. Deer. Oh, no, indeed. They're angels. Well, they have decided to sing on Christmas Eve. They want to do a song at every house, but they can't decide on a song.

Mrs. Santa. They will be visiting an awful lot of houses. I would suggest a short song. (*She might suggest a currently popular number.*)

Mrs. Deer. They want a song with a ring to it.

Mrs. Santa. Then the ideal song is "Jingle Bells."

Mrs. Deer. How perfect. You are a dear. (*Kisses* Mrs. Santa *and exits.*)

Murgatroyd. (*Runs in with letters.*) The latest mail. More toy orders for Santa!

Mrs. Santa. Thank you, Murgatroyd.

Murgatroyd. You're welcome. Now, back to the toy room! (*He leaves.*)

Mrs. Santa. Santa, Santa Claus. Today's mail is here!

Santa (*entering in shirt and suspenders*). Good, good. Ho, ho, ho, I love to read the mail. Aha, this one is from a little girl in Kansas named Dorothy. She wants a dog collar and a new pair of shoes. Red, of course. Here's one from a strange place, Creepy Castle, Haunted Hilltop, U.S.A., Zip Code 000 Uh-Oh—and a half.

Mrs. Santa. Now, who would have an address like that?

Santa. Let's see. (*Reads.*) Dear Santa Claus, if there really is a you. My friend Bah Humbug says there is no Santa Claus. If you will answer my letter, that will prove you are real. Please answer. Yours anxiously, Witchie. Hmmmm, Witchie,—I've never been to her Creepy Castle.

Mrs. Santa. What are you going to do about this, Santa?

Santa. Answer her letter, of course. I can't have anyone thinking there is no Santa Claus, can I?

Mrs. Santa. Certainly not. Santa, I have an idea. Why don't you invite Witchie to come and visit us here at the North Pole. Then she can see for herself that you are real.

Santa. A marvelous idea, Momma. I'll get my pen and—

Mrs. Santa. I must see about the peppermint candies. (*Exits.*)

Santa. Here's my pen. Think I'll write her a postcard. Now, let's see, her name and address (*Writes.*)—Miss Witchie, Creepy Castle, Haunted Hilltop, U.S.A., Zip Code 000 Uh-Oh and a half. (*Turns card over.*) Dear Witchie, Mrs. Claus and I would like for you to come and visit us before Christmas. You'll have no trouble finding us. It's the big house at the North Pole. Hope to see you soon. Love, Santa. There now. Hmmmm, with all the mail and the Christmas rush, she might not get this for weeks. I'll send it special delivery. Seems I remember putting a special delivery stamp in my desk drawer. I'll get it. (*Exits.*)

DANCER (*dancing in*). Anything to go to the post office? Any packages? Any letters? Aha, here's a postcard, all addressed and everything. Creepy Castle, funny place. I'll take it and mail it for Santa. (*Exits.*)

SANTA (*returning*). I have the special delivery stamp, where's the postcard? I left it right here. I'm certain I left it here. Momma, did you get my postcard?

MRS. SANTA (*entering*). No, dear, I've been in the candy kitchen.

SANTA. I left it here when I went to get the stamp, and now it has disappeared. Who could have taken it?

MRS. SANTA. I did see Dancer running toward the post office. Isn't that thoughtful of him to mail it for you?

SANTA. Oh, no. I wanted it to go special delivery. If Witchie doesn't get it in time she won't believe in me. If there is even one person who does not believe in Santa Claus, it ruins my Christmas.

MRS. SANTA. Now, Santa, don't get upset. Surely she'll get the postcard.

SANTA. I certainly hope so.

MRS. SANTA. Try not to worry about it. You have all these orders to fill. Come, I'll help you. (*They exit.*)

(Curtain)

119

Act III

SCENE. *Back at Creepy Castle*

WITCHIE (*pacing the floor*). It has been so long since I wrote to Santa Claus, and no answer. Here it is the day before Christmas. If I don't hear today, then I'll have to admit that Bah Humbug is right. There is no Santa Claus. (*Tries to hold back a sob as the two penguins appear at the far end of the castle and ring the bell.*) Now, who can that be? I'm not expecting anyone. Come in. (*Penguins enter.*)

FIRST PENGUIN. Pardon me, is this the South Pole?

WITCHIE. The South Pole. Heavens, no! This is Creepy Castle.

SECOND PENGUIN. It's cold enough to be the South Pole.

FIRST PENGUIN. It feels like home.

WITCHIE. I'm glad you like it here. Won't you birds sit down?

SECOND PENGUIN. Where is the fireplace?

WITCHIE. You're standing in it.

FIRST PENGUIN. Oh! Thank goodness, there's no fire in it.

WITCHIE. A pity, really. I could do with a roast penguin. Ha, ha, ha, ha. Forgive me, that was just a little hungry humor. Would you care for a frozen icicle?

SECOND PENGUIN. No, thank you. We had better be on our way, or we'll miss the Christmas party at the South Pole. Can you tell us which way is south?

WITCHIE. You go down the hill and—No, you go over the hill—no, er ask a Boy Scout—or get a compass of your own. Lots of luck.

FIRST PENGUIN. Thanks. (*Starts waddling.*)

SECOND PENGUIN. This time I'll lead the way. (*They exit.*)

WITCHIE. Poor penguins. They'll never make it to the South Pole in time for the party, unless they take an Antarctic tern (*Cackles.*) or catch a jet-powered gull. (BAH HUMBUG *enters and rings bell.*) That can only be the ring of doom. Come in, Bah Humbug.

BAH (*entering*). How did you know it was I?

WITCHIE. It's about time for you to show up and say "I told you so."

BAH. Then you have not heard from your, heh, heh, Santa Claus?

120

WITCHIE. Not yet. But it's not too late for a special delivery.

BAH. Bah, humbug! I told you there was no Santa Claus. You won't get an answer.

GHOST (*appearing, and speaking in a quivery voice*). Hi, there. (BAH *jumps.*)

WITCHIE. Ghost, I told you to stay out of sight when company is here.

GHOST. Who is company?

BAH. I am.

GHOST (*turning to Bah*). Oh, you. (*Turns toward* WITCHIE, *then quickly back to* BAH.) Boo!

BAH (*jumping two feet backward*). Don't do that!

WITCHIE. Ghost, behave yourself.

BAH. Be a good little Ghostie or Santa won't come to see you. Bah!

GHOST. Boo! (BAH *jumps again.*)

WITCHIE. Ghost, do you remember the other day, when I went out and left you here alone? (GHOST *nods.*) Did the mailman come and bring anything?

GHOST. What mailman?

WITCHIE. The postman. The one who never stops here, the man in the mailman suit. Think! (*Pushes Ghost's nose.*) Think harder! (*Pushes the nose more.*) Think, Ghost. (*Pushes his nose inside his face.*) Oh dear, look what I've done. Ghost, can't you keep a straight face when I'm talking to you? (GHOST *mutters.*) Stop that muttering.

BAH. What do you do in a case like this?

WITCHIE. I usually pull his ear. (*Pulls* GHOST's *ear.*) Maybe I should pull the other ear. (*Pulls.*) The top of the head? (*Taps* GHOST's *head.*) Nothing there.

BAH. Let me tap him.

WITCHIE. No, no. Ah, now I remember. Boo! (GHOST's *nose pops out.*)

GHOST. Thanks.

WITCHIE. Now concentrate. Did someone leave a piece of mail here?

GHOST. What's mail?

WITCHIE. A letter or postcard; a thing about this big, with writing on it. Think.

GHOST. I'm thinking.

WITCHIE. Think harder. (*Pushes his nose.*)

GHOST. You're pushing my nose again. Do you want me to lose face in front of him?

WITCHIE. Sorry, but please think. (GHOST *turns toward* BAH.) Ahh-haaa, don't do it. (GHOST *looks back to* WITCHIE.) Think, dear.

GHOST (*turning quickly to* BAH). Boo! (BAH *jumps.*)

BAH. He caught me off guard again.

WITCHIE. Again? As usual is more like it. Try to remember about the mail, Ghost.

BAH. What's the use of all this? No mailman came here.

GHOST. Wait, I remember a man with a mustache—

WITCH. The mailman.

GHOST. Last Thursday—

WITCHIE. That's when I went downtown to look at the Christmas decorations. Ghostie, did he leave anything?

GHOST. Whooooo?

WITCHIE. The mailman! Honestly, there are times—

GHOST. Seems to me there was a little card—

WITCHIE. A postcard. Where is it? (*Points toward* GHOST's *nose.*)

GHOST. I put it someplace.

WITCHIE. Where?

GHOST. I don't remember. Ahh-haaa, don't push my nose.

WITCHIE. Then think. You're not thinking hard enough.

GHOST. Behind the door.

BAH. What door?

GHOST. Over there.

WITCHIE. This door? Oh, here it is, a postcard. The postmark says the North Pole. It's addressed to Miss Witchie, Creepy Castle. It's for me Oh, Bah Humbug, it's for me.

BAH. Don't stand there moaning and groaning, read it?

WITCHIE. Dear Witchie. Mrs. Claus and I would like for you to come and visit us before Christmas. You'll have no trouble finding us. It's the big house at the North Pole. Hope to see you soon. L-O-V-E, Santa. L-O-V-E what's that? (*If the audience does not respond,* BAH *should.*) Love! You mean Santa Claus loves me? Oh, Bah Humbug, there is a Santa Claus, and he loves me. Now do you believe?

BAH. Well, I suppose so. Are you going to accept his invitation?

WITCHIE. Of course! It would be unladylike not to. Oh, what shall I wear?

BAH. Anything but what you have on now. You look a mess.

WITCHIE. I didn't know you had noticed.

BAH. Why don't you wear your Halloween costume?

WITCHIE. Good thought. Excuse me. (*Exits.*)

GHOST. May I be excused?

BAH. I'll excuse you, but I'll never forgive you.

GHOST (*turning quickly*). Boo! (BAH *jumps.* GHOST *exits chuckling ghostishly.*)

BAH. One of these days—

WITCHIE (*entering, in fancy dress*). How do I look?

BAH. Like a witch. Heh, heh, how are you traveling?

WITCHIE. By magic broom, of course. Broom! Come here, dear broom. (BROOM *appears but stays out of reach. There is much byplay as she tries to coax the broom within grabbing distance.*) Broom, we are going to the North Pole (BROOM *shrieks* "No, no!") Yes, yes. ("No, no!") You always enjoy flying, Broom. Why not the North Pole? ("*Coooooold!*") Oh, I forgot to give the broom his antifreeze.

BAH. Antifreeze for a broom?

WITCHIE. Come, Broom, dear. (BROOM *is reluctant, but* WITCHIE *grabs him.*) I've got you. Antifreeze time. (*Takes the broom out.*)

BAH. Now I've seen everything. This is ridiculous. (BROOM *lets out a long moan, bursts onto the stage, and bangs his stick against the floor and walls, and against* BAH.)

WITCHIE. (*Runs in.*) Now we're ready to fly. See you later, Bah Humbug. (*Throws her skirts around the broomstick.*)

BAH. Watch out for flying saucers, and satellites!

WITCHIE. Off we go! (*Flies off.*)

BAH. Santa Claus? Christmas? Bah, humbug!

(Curtain)

Act IV

SCENE. *Santa's Home*

SANTA. Momma, any word from the witch?

MRS. SANTA. No, dear.

SANTA. She didn't get my card, she didn't get our invitation.

MRS. SANTA. Don't fret yourself, Santa. You did all you could.

SANTA. Here it is Christmas Eve, and she hasn't arrived. This means she won't be here, and she won't believe in me, and—

MRS. SANTA. There, there, it just can't be helped. It's time for you to get dressed in your warm clothing, dear. I have your coat and cap out on your bed; and your boots and mittens are there by your chair.

SANTA. Oh, dear, dear me—(*Exits.*)

OLD ELFRIEDA (*backing up the stairs*). Mrs. Claus, Mrs. Santa Claus. Where are you?

MRS. SANTA. Here I am, Old Elfrieda.

OLD ELFRIEDA. I hear you, but I don't see you.

MRS. SANTA. I'm right behind you, dear.

OLD ELFRIEDA. Where? Oops! (*Knocks* MRS. CLAUS *down again.*) Mrs. Claus, what are you doing on the floor again? Here, let me help you up.

MRS. SANTA. Thank you. What is it now?

OLD ELFRIEDA. I can't find the yellow doll dresses. I looked high— (*Goes through looking motions.*)

MRS. SANTA. And low—

OLD ELFRIEDA. On the table—

MRS. SANTA. And under the table—

OLD ELFRIEDA. In the drawers—

MRS. SANTA. And on the shelves—

BOTH TOGETHER. No yellow doll dresses anywhere.

MRS. SANTA. Old Elfrieda, where do you usually find the yellow doll dresses?

OLD ELFRIEDA. On the dolls wearing the—wearing the yellow doll dresses. Of course!

Mrs. Santa. Exactly, dear, and the dolls are already in Santa's pack. You put them there this morning.

Old Elfrieda. Yes-s-s-s, now I remember. Well, in that case I'll not fall down the stairs. (*Goes down out of sight.*)

Mrs. Santa. What do you know! She didn't fall!

Old Elfreida. (*Runs back up.*) You thought I was going to fall, but I fooled you, didn't I? (*Turns and falls.*) Oops! (*She disappears and the two reindeer run in.*)

Dancer. Mrs. Claus.

Mrs. Santa. Shouldn't you two be in harness?

Dancer. First we have to sing for you.

Prancer. We've been practicing so hard.

Mrs. Santa. Well, hurry, boys, Santa is putting on his coat.

Dancer. Ready, Prancer?

Prancer. Ready, Dancer?

Dancer. A-one, a-two—(*They sing "Jingle Bells," Dancer singing the verse, Prancer the chorus—but at the same time.*)

Mrs. Santa. Hold it, hold it. Prancer, you shouldn't be singing the chorus while Dancer sings the verse.

Prancer. Right. Shall we try it again, Dancer?

Dancer. Naturally. We want to do this right. A-one, a-two—(*This time Dancer sings the chorus and Prancer sings the verse, both at the same time.*)

Mrs. Santa. I give up. Along with you two, out to the sleigh.

Prancer. And away we go. (*They exit singing, "Deck the Halls."*)

Irmatrude. (*Runs in with a teddy bear.*) Here's the last teddy bear. One ear was sewed on backwards, and I had to change it.

Mrs. Santa. Put it in Santa's pack, Irmatrude.

Irmatrude. Right away. He should be leaving, it's getting late. (*Exits.*)

Mrs. Santa. Santa, hurry, dear.

Santa (*entering, in coat and hat*). I'm ready. Is my pack ready?

Mrs. Santa. (*Brings in his big pack.*) It's packed to overflowing. I'll put it here for the brownies to load in the sleigh. (*Puts it out of sight.*) There will be lots of happy boys and girls tomorrow morning, Santa.

126

SANTA. No sign of Witchie?

MRS. SANTA. No. I'm sorry, Santa, you can't wait any longer. You have a long trip.

SANTA. You're right. Well, I suppose there's—(*Witchie flies in and lands kerplop on top of Santa Claus.*)

WITCHIE. Whoops! Sorry! The broom almost missed the back door. Oh (*Realizes she's on top of* SANTA, *but can't remember his name.*), I know you. You're—you're—you're, oh, I've seen your picture on Christmas cards and everywhere. You're—now don't tell me—I'll get it. Those laughing eyes—why aren't your eyes laughing?

SANTA. I can't get my breath.

WITCHIE. Those dimples. Those beard—I mean, whiskers! And—and you're so jolly, and—oh, I could never forget who you are. You're, oh, if only I could remember your name—

MRS. SANTA. Will you please get off him. Santa has to leave.

WITCHIE. Santa, that's who you are. I knew it all the time. Santa Lucia?

Santa Domingo? Santa Barbara? Oh, I'm so thrilled to meet you at last. I'm so excited—

MRS. SANTA. Please let Santa Claus up.

WITCHIE. Santa Claus. Of course. Why, Santa, you shouldn't be on the floor at a time like this! You should be in your sleigh and on your way. Here, let me dust you off. (*Pulls* SANTA *up and brushes him off.*) And to think you're Santa Claus.

SANTA. I knew it all the time.

WITCHIE. I'm Witchie. Forgive me for being so shy, but I'm so thrilled I'm speechless. Oh, you're real. (*Touches* SANTA.) You're really real. And I believe in you—oh, I do, I really do.

SANTA. I'm glad, but really I must be going now.

WITCHIE. Of course you must.

MRS. SANTA. Have a good trip, dear.

SANTA. I will, Momma. (*Kisses her good-bye.*)

WITCHIE. Good-bye, Santa. (*Grabs him and gives him a big bear hug and kiss.*)

SANTA. Good-bye, goodbye. (*Exits.*)

WITCHIE. He's just what I expected him to be, plump and soft and lovable.

MRS. SANTA. You arrived just in time, Witchie. He was so afraid you hadn't received his card.

WITCHIE. Actually, I didn't stand a ghost of a chance of getting it, but I did. Well, here I am, and there you are. Hi there.

MRS. SANTA. Would you like to see the workrooms?

WITCHIE. Would I? You bet. I want to see all the pretty dolls in their red dresses and blue dresses and yellow dresses—

MRS. SANTA. Oh, I just remembered, The dolls are all with Santa.

WITCHIE. Well, actually I adore boy-toys. Let's see the workshop!

MRS. SANTA. It's empty, too.

WITCHIE. And the candy kitchen—don't tell me, it's empty, too.

MRS. SANTA. I'm afraid so. I'm so sorry.

WITCHIE. Don't give it another thought.

MURGATROYD (*entering with a stack of letters*). Here are the last-minute letters for Santa. I hope he has enough toys left to fill these orders. (*Runs off.*)

Mrs. Santa. Oh, no, Santa is already on his way.

Witchie. And the boys and girls who wrote these letters will be disappointed.

Mrs. Santa. This is terrible. Santa will be so upset. He hates to disappoint anyone. But there are no toys left.

Witchie. Now, hold on just a toy-making minute. I still have a magic power or two left.

Mrs. Santa. I don't understand.

Witchie. Stand back, give me room. I'll put the letters here. Now, I'll concentrate. "Powers of good, do as you should! Provide the toys for these girls and boys. With magic speed do your deed, and if you don't—just remember, I have a temper! Kerflammm!" (*A bag of toys appears.*)

Mrs. Santa. How wonderful! But, Witchie, Santa is on his way. He must be over Canada by now. How will we get these toys to him?

Witchie. I'll catch him. I'll take the toys to him on my magic broom. Come, Broom. (*Broom appears.*), We're flying to catch Santa. (*Broom groans, "No, no."*) Yes, yes. ("*No, no!*") Do you want more antifreeze? ("*No, I'll go.*") Good. (*Hooks the bag loop over the broomstick.*)

Mrs. Santa. Wait, Witchie. (*Dashes off and dashes back with the box or basket with air holes.*) Take this. Tell Santa it's for the last stop.

WITCHIE. The last stop, right!

MRS. SANTA. Good luck! And thank you, my dear.

WITCHIE. Glad to help. 'Bye now. Off we go (*Flies off.*)

(Curtain)

The cast at the North Pole gathers for a group portrait

Act V

SCENE. *Creepy Castle. Everything is gloomy.* WITCHIE *and* SANTA *enter.*

WITCHIE. What an awful place, so gloomy and dismal. There's certainly no Christmas spirit here.

SANTA. This is our last stop.

WITCHIE. I pity anyone who lives in a place like this.

SANTA. Take a good look, Witchie.

WITCHIE. Hmmmm, it looks familiar. Oh, no, this is where I live!

SANTA. Then you know where the kitchen is. Could you fix us up something warm?

WITCHIE. You bet. I'll whip up a little witch's brew in no time.

SANTA. Hot tea or hot chocolate would be fine, nothing elaborate.

WITCHIE. You're the boss. Now, where did I leave the kitchen? Oh, yes, right in the middle of the raspberry pizza. (*Exits.*)

SANTA. Now to get some Christmas spirit in here. I'll need my long stick. (*Gets the stick and proceeds to hang silver tinsel in loops across the castle. As he finishes* BAH HUMBUG *comes in. The lights grow brighter.*)

BAH. Anybody home?

SANTA. Come in. Merry Christmas!

BAH. Bah, humbug!

SANTA. Glad to meet you. I'm Santa Claus. Witchie has told me a lot about you.

BAH. She has? You are? I mean—er, er—you really are, aren't you?

SANTA. Certainly. I wonder if you would lend me a hand? Could you rustle up some wood for the fireplace there?

BAH. Witchie never has a fire, never.

SANTA. Wood, please, and lots of it. I'd like a big, roaring fire, such as Creepy Castle has never seen.

BAH. (*Goes off, comes back immediately with the andirons and fire.*) Does this suit you?

SANTA. Perfectly. A beautiful fire. (*The lights grow warm on the stage.*) Oh, Witchie, would you bring me the basket for the last stop. It's still in the sleigh.

WITCHIE (*offstage*). Sure thing, Santa. (*Enters.*) Here it is.

SANTA. Open it.

WITCHIE. But it's for the last stop.

SANTA. And this is it. It's for you.

WITCHIE. For me? I've never had a gift before. (*Opens and takes out a kitten.*) Oh, a kitten. I've never had a kitten.

SANTA. Every witch should have a cat, and this little fellow will be a cat one day.

WITCHIE. Oh, thank you, Santa—and Mrs. Claus. My first Christmas present.

BAH. Kitten, present, bah, humbug!

SANTA. Bah, for you. (*Gives him the beautifully wrapped package.*) Now don't open it until morning. That's part of the fun, you know, wondering what's in a package.

BAH. A present, for me? I don't know what to say.

WITCHIE. Try "thank you," Bah.

BAH. Oh, of course. Thank you, Santa Claus.

SANTA. You're welcome. Now, I must be on my way home. I always have Christmas breakfast with Momma, then she lets me sleep for two days and three nights. Ho, ho, ho, thank you for your help, Witchie. And you know what, I believe in *you*. Ho, ho, ho. Merry Christmas! (*Exits.*)

WITCHIE and BAH. Merry Christmas, Santa!

WITCHIE. Drive carefully.

BAH. What if he falls asleep? He looks awfully tired.

WITCHIE. The reindeer know the way home. Bah, don't go home. Let's have a party. Creepy Castle has never had a party.

BAH. It would be better than going back to my lonely little hut.

WITCHIE. It's not much of a party with just two— (*The two penguins wander in.*)

FIRST PENGUIN. Pardon me, but is this—a Christmas Party?

SECOND PENGUIN. A Christmas Party!

WITCHIE. It is. And you're both invited. Pull up a pinfeather and sit down.

FIRST PENGUIN. Thank you. This isn't the South Pole, but it's a lot nicer.

WITCHIE. You bet it is. This is Christmas at Creepy Castle! (*Hugs the kitten.*)

(Curtain)

Note: Among the colored photographs which follow many are from plays not included in this book. The pictures are shown to give the reader an idea of the Tichenor costumes and stage settings.

Two of the Tichenor puppets for the Broadway musical "Carnival"

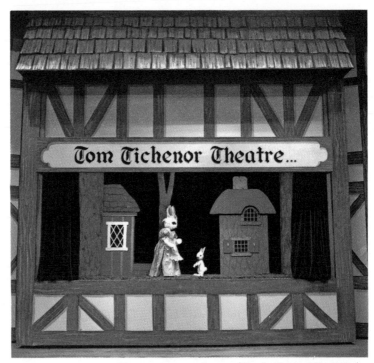

The marionette theater, Nashville Public Library

"Jack and the Beanstalk"

"Why the Bear Has a Stumpy Tail"

Hand puppets above are from Tichenor's "Why the Hen Didn't Cackle," a children's concert—music and pantomime for actors, puppets, and orchestra

On the opposite page are scenes from Tichenor's production of "Bremen Town Musicians"

IV
MARIONETTES

Marionettes are the problem puppets where perseverance, patience, and practice are required, all three in large quantities. Marionettes take considerably longer to make than hand puppets. Much more of the work in construction and costuming has to be done by hand. But, like most things that take hard work, a really good marionette show brings a degree of satisfaction that makes all the effort worthwhile.

I always advise everyone to work with hand puppets before attempting marionettes. One needs experience in construction, planning, and performing first. Once you have a good basic puppet background, you are better prepared to enter the world of strings. You will find in the instructional sections of this book many references to hand-puppet methods, because marionette parts are often made the very same way.

HEADS

Of all the materials I've worked with, I prefer cloth for heads As a rule I try to use a complete cast of cloth-head marionettes or a cast of modeled heads, not mixing the two except in rare cases. This gives each play its own special look. And it gives variety to the repertoire with no two consecutive productions looking the same.

CLOTH. Cloth heads for marionettes are made the same way basically as for hand puppets, only a neck is added. I recommend using wire to carry the weight of the body. Run the wire from ear to ear and down through the neck. This will keep the head and neck from stretching out of shape. Sew the wire down across the back of the head. Twist a small loop in the wire above each ear for the head strings, and at the bottom of the neck where a wire loop will join it to the body wire.

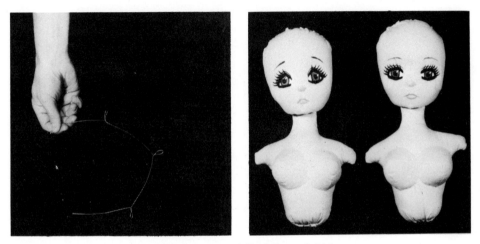

See also pages 140, 141, and 144

CAST PLASTIC WOOD. The original head is modeled in clay. A plaster cast is made in two parts, the front and the back. This calls for boxes to contain the plaster. The clay head is greased with petroleum jelly and pushed face down into the wet plaster. When the plaster hardens, this process is repeated for the back of the head. Remove the clay head carefully. Grease the plaster molds and press in the plastic wood. This will dry more quickly if the first layer is not too thick. When the plastic-wood parts are removed from the molds, they will need to be trimmed carefully and put together with glue or more plastic wood. Most

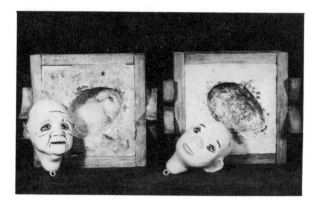

likely the head will need a bit of patching and a lot of sanding. A coat or two of acrylic gesso will help smooth out the surface and make the flesh-color paint go on more smoothly.

You will notice in the photographs that several of the girl-marionettes have upper torsos of plastic wood. This calls for more plaster molds. I must confess that my brother made the molds for me years ago, and they have been used over and over. Most of the plastic-wood heads were cast in molds made of latex rubber. The rubbermolds enabled me to cast heads with deep undercuts in noses, ears, and such. When the rubber molds are made thin enough to peel off easily they have to rest in a box with soft cotton so the heads won't dry lopsided.

About half of my human marionette heads are made of plastic wood. They can be more realistic than cloth heads, and the only real problem I ever had with them was that I was forever scratching the paint. They were made before acrylic paints were popular, and now I face the rather monumental task of repainting at least one hundred heads, not to mention cleaning and refurbishing the costumes.

PAPER-MACHE. The new prepared paper-mache makes durable heads. The heads need not be solid. They will dry more quickly if they are hollow. They can be made in the same casts as the plastic-wood heads, or they can be modeled over some sort of base. This will make them lighter, and less expensive too. Two longtime suggestions for bases are light bulbs and styrofoam balls.

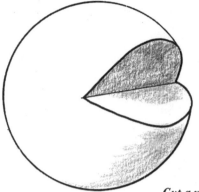

Cut a v-shaped groove across the middle of a styrofoam ball

STYROFOAM-BALL AND CLOTH HEADS. I have experimented with making heads from the lightweight styrofoam balls. With a butcher knife cut a V-shaped groove across the middle of the ball. This is the eye trench.

Cut a circle of peach-colored cloth big enough to cover the entire ball. Run a thread around the edge of the circle. Put a layer of cotton over the front of the ball, keeping the eye trench in the center. Then put the

141

The witch from Tichenor's production of "Jorinda and Joringel"

cloth circle over it and pull it together in the back with the thread.

Make the cloth nose, stuff it firmly, pin it in place, and sew it on.

Next, wire the head as you would a cloth head. Run wires through the head from side to side and down to the neck, with loops twisted at the ends for stringing.

Now for the eyes. Cut out the felt pieces. Before gluing them together, cut holes in the centers, so the back of the eye-button will recess into the layers of felt. Glue the felt pieces together. When the pieces dry, run a wire from the button through the felt and then through the head. When both eyes are in place, pull the wire tighter so the eyes will sink into the cotton-padded eye trench, giving more contour to the face. (You might try this type of head on a hand puppet after using a corer to make the finger hole.)

A styrofoam head made this way is best for characters with beards, such as giants, dwarfs, and old men. The beard disguises the ball shape.

There are other materials available for heads: Celastic, paper towels and paste, felt, and—one of the oldest—carved wood. When felt is used, it should have a lining of woven cloth or it will soon stretch and pull apart.

142

BODIES

Bodies made of cloth are by far the easiest to make (and costume). The bodies can be made in one piece, or jointed at the waist. Most of my marionettes with waist joints are girls having upper torsos of plastic wood. The joint is good for a clown or a dancer who needs the extra flexibility. The jointed body has a tendency to make the marionette slump when sitting and undulate unduly while walking.

If the marionette head is heavy, a bit of weight may be needed in the lower body to counterbalance it.

ARMS. The arms should be weighted at the wrists if the hands are to be joined loosely. Weights may be bits of lead covered with cotton and inserted at the wrist. If the hands are to be firmly attached to the arm, then the weight should be placed in the hand for maximum benefit. Sew each arm on both sides, leaving the ends open. (Machine stitching saves time.) Turn and sew each elbow seam. Stuff the arms from both ends and sew up the ends by hand. Or you might prefer stitching up the side and across the top of each arm turning and stuffing it to the elbow, hand-stitching across the arms at the elbow seam, and stuffing to the wrist. This gives the arm a real shoulder movement. I add an elbow pad so the arm will have more shape when bent.

Try the arms at different positions before sewing them to the body. Just remember that a marionette that cannot move is merely a doll, and not a performer.

HANDS. Making hands can be a real headache. I make mine of peach-colored cloth. I sew them on the machine with a fine stitch. I then turn them, insert wire skeletons, and stuff them with cotton. Making hands this way is difficult; I nearly go berserk. But such hands have the right look to go with my heads. You can make them if you persist. I clip the cloth between the fingers before turning. I use a long mattress needle for turning and stuffiing. Pipe cleaners take the place of both wire and cotton for stuffing hands. It usually takes two or more pipe cleaners bent double to fill a finger and make it hold its shape when bent.

I almost hesitate to make the next suggestion, but the advent of soft

143

plastic dolls makes it too tempting to pass over. If your heroine's hands pose too big a problem, go to the nearest Goodwill or Salvation Army store and buy several dolls with good hands. Examine them carefully to be certain the little finger has not been chewed off.

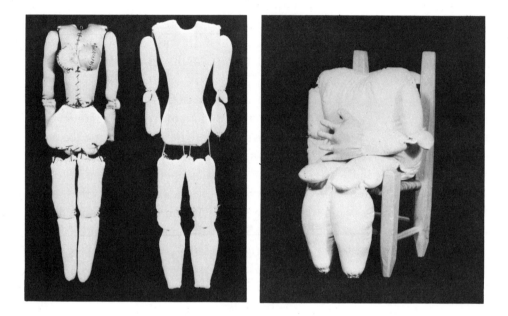

The doll hands can be sewed firmly on the marionette arm to remain rigid, or sewed loosely to bend. Stringing will not be a problem because of the softness of the plastic. The hands can be weighted with bits of lead covered with cotton, wired, and stuffed. Delicate hands do much to add an air of grace to a girl-marionette.

I dismantled a tiny doll, gave her flexible joints, and used her for Thumbelina. She worked beautifully, and looked far more fragile than anything I could have made on such a small scale.

Legs and Feet. Legs can be sewn the same way as arms. Add kneecaps (the same as the elbow pads) to the male characters. Placed correctly, kneecaps will also keep legs from buckling backwards.

I prefer to put weights in the bottoms of the feet, or shoes, since the shoe is the foot. Of course, if you have a barefoot character, then make the foot of flesh-colored cloth and sew on graduated toes, and the result will be very effective.

Sew the shoe top to the bottom, but leave the back end open. Turn and slide in innersoles cut from cardboard. I find it easier to cut about three innersoles of lightweight cardboard for each shoe instead of a single thick one (mainly because you often cut them too large and have to trim them down a bit and thick cardboard is difficult to cut).

Stuff the toes and stuff lightly around the sides of the shoe. Put in the weights and complete the stuffing. Sew up the rear seam of the shoe.

When you sew the shoe to the leg depends on the costume. If the man wears stockings and knee pants, tights, or slender trousers, you have to costume him first and add the shoes later. The same holds true for girl-marionettes.

Not all girl-marionettes need legs and feet. I use hoop skirts or floor-length costumes whenever possible. It makes for easier manipulation and always looks graceful on the stage.

COSTUMES

A marionette costume is not a doll dress. Very seldom do you make an outfit and slip it onto a figure. Most costumes have to be made in several pieces and then sewn directly to the body. The marionette's flexibility calls for this approach. Sleeves should be loose enough to let the elbow bend easily. Pants should allow the marionette to walk and sit without difficulty, and yet not be baggy.

Marionettes work best in soft materials: lightweight woolens, jerseys, silks and satins, muslin, and velveteen. Use heavy brocades only for parts of a costume that do not have to bend. The same goes for burlap, upholstery fabrics, and the like. I once dressed a princess in flocked taffeta. She could not walk or sit, but she certainly could wrinkle! Felt

From the Tichenor productions of (upper) "The Moon Maiden"
and (lower) "Puss in Boots"

From the Tichenor productions of "Cinderella" and "Rapunzel"

is fine for hats, shoes, and trimming, and if it is lightweight it can be used for jackets.

There aren't any hard and fast *don'ts* in costuming. Just keep in mind what the character must do on stage. If the part calls for a stiff, pompous person who is unbending, why not use stiff, unbending fabrics that will help him maintain the correct demeanor.

Even ragged clothes should be designed or planned. A coat or dress should show what it is, no matter how poor the wearer. A hank of rags means nothing. A shredded sleeve, a tattered jacket, a few patches will give the worn-out effect better. Patches need not be of the crazy-quilt variety. My Cinderella wears a brown dress with patches in shades of brown and tan in varying textures. The costume is much more in character than it would be with floral print and striped patches.

Don't be afraid to use odd color combinations in the costumes. These days there seem to be no new combinations left to call "odd."

My favorite costume periods are the medieval (the really romantic, fairy-tale look), the eighteenth century (perukes, kneepants, and panniers), and the 1850s (hoopskirts). Illustrators have always been prone to mix periods. Often—especially in readers and fairy tale books—you will see

147

Left, the queen from "Rumpelstiltskin" and, right, the fairy godmother from "Cinderella"

a king in ermine-trimmed robe, tights, buckle shoes, and with a ruff around his neck. His queen will sport a hoopskirt, pointed hennin, and a powdered wig, all the while looking at the world through her lorgnette. You will find more satisfaction, and give a more professional look to your production, if you adhere to one period at a time in your designs. Absolute authenticity is not necessary; an overall impression is.

A friend once coined a word to described the style and period in many of my shows: peasantine. Rather an apt word, signifying full skirts, aprons, ruffles and braid, velveteen jackets, felt boots, laced girdles and full sleeves, embroidered suspenders, and lots of petticoats.

Whatever the style or period, keep the lines uncluttered and the trim bold enough to be seen. Don't overdress the puppet. Don't let the costume restrict movement. Avoid buttons and brittle trimming in places where strings will catch. Hide the neck joint with a collar, kerchief, or necklace. All joints are unattractive. Give them freedom, but keep them as inconspicuous as possible.

*The goat with "One Eye, Two Eyes, Three Eyes" as produced
by Tom Tichenor*

MARIONETTE CONTROLS

Being of a nonmechanical bent and an archaic frame of mind, I have
stuck with the same basic control that I first used. There have been
minor changes—chiefly, it is smaller. It does the job for me, and is
often called the airplane control.

The piece you hold in your left hand has screw eyes at the front for
the hand strings, at the other end for the back strings, and just past the
middle for the shoulders. The short crosspiece supports the head. The
foot bar which you work with your right hand has a hole in the middle
to fit over the dowel, which is rounded at the top.

This is as simple a control as can be, yet it makes possible the basic
movements.

See text, page 149

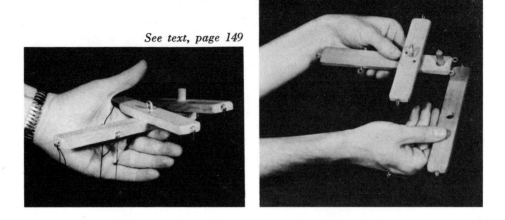

STRINGING. I rig up a wire in a doorway to hold the control while stringing it. The control should be at the working height you use on stage. Start with the head strings, one at each ear. It is easier if you can have someone hold the marionette while you run the strings from the head to the control. This will prevent an irritating session of tying and untying.

The shoulder strings are done next. I put them slightly down on the back, not on top of the shoulders. Put them close enough together so the head will not fall backward through them.

The back string is attached at the back center of the seat. The positioning of strings varies, depending on the individual movement desired. A string coming from the center of the back of the hand will give a flat movement. A string from the palm makes a picking-up movement. I put the string between the thumb and the forefinger for a natural look.

You may have noticed in the photographs that a black thread runs from the tip of the thumb through the tip of each finger across to the little finger. This is to keep the leg strings from catching on the fingers (which can cause minor calamities).

Leg strings come from the top of the knees generally. If a man has to cross his legs, put the string on his shin. The leg strings should be a tiny bit longer than the others so that the foot bar can be lifted off the control without moving the legs.

I use heavy, black nylon thread from a shoe company for stringing. You may use button thread. Some puppeteers like nylon fishline, but I find it too stiff. I like the security of a strong thread, and I always use black. If the thread tends to slip—and nylon will—touch the knot with a bit of glue.

A typical marionette has nine strings. This enables it to make all the ordinary movements. Unusual actions may require an extra string or two. Each additional string is an added nuisance. A girl with a hoopskirt needs no legs or leg strings. On the other hand, if she has to pick up her skirt, you can run a string from the skirt (preferably from where her hand rests naturally) through a loop between her fingers, up to the control. It should be slack enough so the arm can move naturally with the original hand string.

Once the marionette has its strings it is subject to the direst calamity of all: tangles! A prime rule for working with marionettes must be obeyed faithfully—it should become second nature to you. It is this: pick up the marionette by its control, not by its body or head. When you put the marionette down, put the control on top of its body or by its head. Never, never grab the marionette first. The control will turn more flips than you ever thought possible, and the nine strings, will tangle into a Gordian knot.

When you have a tangled marionette never throw it on the floor in disgust. That only compounds the problem. A cool head can usually work out the tangles without having to untie a single string.

MANIPULATION. If you are right-handed, hold the control in your left hand, your forefinger under the bar between the head bar and the shoulder strings. This should be the balance point with the marionette hanging straight and relaxed. Put your thumb on top of the control. Pull the little finger back until it creates a pressure on the shoulder strings. Tilt the control down slightly at the front. You are forcing the weight from the head strings to the shoulder strings. Tilt the control from side to side. The

From Tichenor's production "Cinderella Rabbit"

From Tichenor's production "Beauty and the Beast"

From the Tichenor production "The Princess Who Could Not Cry"

From the Tichenor production "The Almost Godfather"

*From the Tichenor productions (top) "Thumbelina" and (bottom)
"Rumpelstiltskin"*

head should swing a bit down and to the side each time. Once you get the feel of this movement, practice making the head shake "no." Make the head look down. With more practice you can control the head without moving the body or making it lean forward. The head movements can be done with the left hand only, leaving the right hand free for other things.

Walking a marionette is not as easy as it looks. Try it on a rug instead of a slick floor. The traction of the feet on the rug is a great help. Otherwise the back leg will slide up when the marionette moves.

Take the foot bar off the dowel with your right hand. Make slow steps at first, with each movement distinct, leaving one leg back as the other goes forward. Advance the body gently. Try leaning the body forward ever so slightly by raising the back of the control. This gives a more natural appearance. You will soon learn that the least movement of the head will add to the realism, as will little gestures of the hand.

A big mistake that many puppeteers make is not holding the body high enough when it is walking. The marionette proceeds across the stage in a sitting position with the legs moving frantically, looking more like a spider than a human. Establish the center of gravity in the body when it is moving. And when a marionette is standing still, keep the feet on the ground and the legs straight. No drooping, please. A puppet should exit as a person would. Only Peter Pan should fly in and out of the wings. Keep the marionette on the floor until it is out of sight of the audience. Amateurs and professionals alike sometimes yank the puppets up before they leave the stage, or they fling them on stage with abandon, perhaps in misguided efforts to keep the show moving. Whatever the reason, it is still shoddy showmanship.

Sitting down correctly is so simple a movement that one wonders why it isn't done properly. Watch someone sit down. Sit down yourself and notice whether this is true: you lean forward as you let yourself down. Getting up you do the same, you lean forward as you rise, straightening up as you stand. Some puppeteers back a marionette up to a chair, pull up on the leg strings, and plop the figure down, leaning it backward. For standing they pull the marionette straight up, defying the laws of gravity, balance, and grace. Save such tricks for ghosts and things, and make your people believable.

A marionette without a moving mouth must make some movement when it speaks. Otherwise, you don't know who is talking. Head and hand movements should be animated according to the speech, but not overdone. Small gestures are preferable. You should reserve the large ones to use when you need to express excitement and confusion.

Just as with hand puppets, it is necessary to know your marionettes. When I first began to make marionettes seriously, I carried two or three of them with me when I went visiting. Old Alfonso would walk around rooms on his peg leg, Elsie would dance gracefuly (mostly with her delicate hands), and Rosa would weep and moan. It is a wonder I was ever invited anywhere again. But I did get to know the marionettes. I learned that each figure has its own balance and its own problems, and that each one must be handled according to its needs. During those months I learned to work instinctively. I could make the puppets do what I wanted without thinking about how to do it. They visually expressed the emotions I was speaking. Their joy and sadness came forth seemingly without effort on my part.

I cannot stress too strongly the importance of getting to know your puppets before starting rehearsals with them. What a help it is to have their emotions at your fingertips. Then the director doesn't have to wait while you figure out a movement that should come without thinking—crying, looking to left and right, running, waving, or being sad or glad.

Rehearsals are complicated enough with all the traffic problems. You should not have to learn manipulation during the precious time allotted for rehearsing the play.

ANIMAL MARIONETTES

The hand-puppet animal heads can be adapted for marionettes. Humanized animals—the ones that walk on their hind legs and act like people—

can have regular marionette bodies, can either be dressed, or covered with fur cloth to match the head. The fur skin should be made loose enough to allow for movements, just like a costume—perhaps even more so, since fur cloth is bulky.

Animals who walk on all fours can be made with a stuffed cloth skeleton covered with loose fur cloth, or with the body and legs cut directly from the fur cloth, and sewn, weighted, and stuffed. Most of mine are made by the latter method. I do have a scrawny cat whose skeleton is copied from that of a real cat. It is uncanny to see the catlike positions that the cat puppet can assume. The spine is foam rubber, and this allows the creature to curl up quite naturally.

For very large animals you want to use styrofoam inside the heads and bodies to lessen the weight.

Dog puppets usually walk away with a show. Most of my dogs have only four strings: two on the head, one at the shoulder, the fourth at the back. Sure the legs flop, but the dog can sit, lope, look sad, lie down, and be affectionate. That's a lot from only four strings.

I like to do familiar stories with animals instead of people. *The Emperor's New Clothes* is done with bears, and, when the emperor is supposed to be bare, he really is! Just do the play straight, with little concession to the animal cast, and it will work out well. Avoid the tendency to be too cute and sticky when using animals.

157

From the Tichenor's production of "The Grasshopper and the Ants"

Cocky Locky and Turkey Lurkey from "Chicken Little" make a guest appearance in Tichenor's production of "Billy Goats Gruff"

From Tichenor's production "Harry and the Tortoise"

THE MARIONETTE STAGE

A marionette stage is decidedly more complicated than one for hand
puppets. I have yet to see a really simple one that can be moved around.
First of all, the stage floor has to be higher than the room floor. Secondly,
the bridge or walkway should be at least six inches higher than the stage
floor; otherwise the strings are so short that when a marionette has to
sit down the puppeteer's hands come into view.

My current stage adapts from marionette stage to hand-puppet stage so
that the same lighting and curtains can be used for both. It is designed for
my specific needs and to fit in a particular place. Each stage has to fill
the special requirements of a particular person or group. Most puppetry
books include plans for stages in varying degrees of complexity. I would
suggest that you study as many different sets of plans as possible before
drawing up your own plans. Visit other puppeteers and try out their stages.

When you build your first stage do not attempt to make it the "Definitive

159

Upper, left, "Little Rabbit Who Wanted Red Wings;" right, "The Twelve Months"; lower, left, "The Plump Princess"; right, "Stay-Home Bunny"

Marionette Stage." Your first time out with it will be a revelation. You'll wonder why you did this and did not do that. Start out with a stage as little and simple as possible, and build a complicated, expensive stage only after you have had some experience in performing.

Ofttimes, little things make a big difference: things such as having the light switches where you can work them from the bridge; seemingly inconsequential things such as taking half the glides off your traverse rod so the curtain will pull back farther and not block so much of the stage.

Just remember that if your stage is horrendous to move and set up you may not have have any energy left for the performance. Tired puppeteers are not likely to put on a topnotch show.

SCENERY

I use lots of painted backdrops. I love blue skies peeping through trees, snow on window mullions, deeply shadowed castle walls, thick trees in a forest, and rows of houses along a street. I like painted scenes—tempera on white sheeting (the starchier the better), sometimes shaded with crayons, sometimes touched with glitter.

One becomes resigned to shadows falling across the blue sky as a marionette walks by. Audiences are seldom critical of such things. The backdrops can be flipped over quickly between scenes, and you're somewhere else.

On the other hand, I also like a plain black backdrop. It minimizes the strings. Set pieces or unusual props are very dramatic in front of black, and costumes stand out like jewels. Dark blue is nice, too.

Each stage needs wings to hide the open sides. For outdoor scenes try using thick tree trunks (painted, not real). Or, for general purposes, cover the wings with the same material used for the curtains. The curtains remain in view all the time, and the wings would be a continuation of the same color. My most recent curtains are green velvet, a color chosen as being most compatible for both indoor and outdoor settings. But in my mind a really glamorous theater always has red velvet curtains with gold fringe and tassels.

Set pieces are things like rock walls, tree stumps, clumps of toadstools, and underground stairs. You can model toadstools out of paper-mache. I used to make toadstools of stuffed cloth, sew them to bases of cloth-covered wood with large nails driven through from the underside to stiffen the stems; but the plastic toadstools now on the market are extremely lifelike and appealing. and I often use them. Scale your toadstools and flowers to your characters, big ones for little animals, little ones when the marionettes are human beings. In a play such as *Thumbelina* make the flora and fauna oversize so Thumbelina will seem all the smaller.

PROPS

Baskets are useful if the marionettes's fingers are strong enough to hold the weight. High-back chairs should be weighted so they won't topple over. Toppling is a problem with any furniture made of cardboard. Make furniture strong enough to take the rough handling of quick scene changes.

My favorite pieces are made of one-inch pine, distressed and stained warm brown instead of painted. They are part of the "fat look" that characterizes so much of my design. I tend to lean toward the sturdy, solid things instead of the slender and delicate.

Objects that go on tables and cupboards can cause great delays in scene changes. This problem is compounded when the furniture is treasured and the accessories are heirlooms. Ideally the small pieces should be glued to the tabletop or shelves so everything can be whisked off at once. The most practical solution is to make the furniture of felt-covered, corrugated cardboard, use inexpensive plastic dishes that can be glued on, and save the antiques for photographs.

Sometimes it is better to build props and furniture for the specific play and moment, rather than to construct something so fine that you hate to risk injuring it. My biggest problem is storage. I undertake every project with a determination to make it a thing of beauty and permanency—everything must last a lifetime. But once it is made where do you put it? Keep your productions simple and avoid these pitfalls. Use expendable props instead of collecting antique miniatures. Of course you will miss all the fun of prowling around junk shops and flea markets, and the old things do have a special look. The answer is, learn how to antique plastic.

SELECTING THE PLAY

Selecting the play for a marionette show is more difficult than choosing a hand-puppet play. You might say it is twice as hard. You can have a puppet on each hand, but it takes two hands to operate a marionette. A puppeteer should never hold two marionettes at once unless it cannot be avoided. One puppet is sure to be inanimate part of the time. Hanging marionettes on hooks onstage is even worse. I have had to do it, but I certainly do not recommend it.

A puppeteer is not necessarily needed for each marionette in the show, but things work best when there is a puppeteer for every marionette onstage at any given time. This calls for much versatility in the puppeteers, and for much thought in selecting the play. It is very awkward when one puppeteer is speaking for two characters and someone else is working one of them.

Unless you're doing a play with a class or large group and everybody has to have a part, I would suggest starting out with relatively simple plays. Marionettes can do things that hand puppets and humans cannot —things like flying, taking funny tumbles, leaping higher than possible— you should take advantage of these abilities.

Remember, too, in choosing a play for a certain age level that older children will still enjoy a "young" story if it is done well. So will grown-ups.

163

With all this in mind I am offering one of my simplest and most popular plays, *The Little Rabbit Who Wanted Red Wings*. It has no crowd scenes, and offers unlimited opportunities for improvisation and additions. You can start with my script and soon make it yours.

THE LITTLE RABBIT WHO WANTED RED WINGS*

Characters

MOTHER RABBIT, a nice lady with an apron (she's always cooking, and burning things)

LITTLE RABBIT, a most appealing little bunny

MRS. GRAY SQUIRREL (CLARICE), the neighborly type,

PROFESSOR GROUNDHOG, a dignified old gentleman whose buttons don't match

PINKNEY GREEN, an elf—either boy or girl—all dressed in pink and green

RED BIRD, must fly nicely

LORELEI PUDDLEDUCK, an effusive duck, who is very sure of herself and her artistic talents

SHIRLEY, a teen-age brown squirrel, dressed prettily

LITTLE RABBIT's *red wings can be made of red sponge rubber, feathers, or felt. They can be attached by Velcro if the rabbit can be manuevered so close to the wishing pond a hand can stick them on unseen, and later, close enough to the scenery for the wings to be pulled off. I have always used a continuous black string running from the rabbit's back up to the control and back, with the wings on it. I pull the string pulley fashion to get the wings on and off. This is, perhaps, a clumsy bit of rigging, but it always has worked.*

---

* Play by Tom Tichenor adapted from a Southern folktale, the best known version of which is by Carolyn Sherwin Bailey, copyright © 1961 by Platt & Munk Company, Inc.

In a play like this the cast can be expanded to include other animal characters, the ones suggested here being merely the ones that I used. Skunks in skirts and raccoons in masks, beavers in fur coats and weasels in waistcoats—almost any forest animal of the smaller variety could be used in place of or in addition to these.

Act I

SCENE. *Outside Rabbit house, with part of* LITTLE RABBIT's *house seen at the right, part of a squirrel's tree house at the left.*

MOTHER RABBIT. Little Rabbit! Where are you!

LITTLE RABBIT. Out here, Mother.

MOTHER RABBIT. What are you doing?

LITTLE RABBIT. Sitting on a toadstool, wishing.

MOTHER RABBIT. That's all you do—wish. Wish for this, wish for that.

LITTLE RABBIT. I like to wish. I wish I had a long, red automobile.

MOTHER RABBIT. That's ridiculous, Little Rabbit. Even if you had one, you couldn't drive it. You're too young.

LITTLE RABBIT. I wish I were old enough to drive a long, red automobile.

MOTHER RABBIT. Wish, wish, wish—I wish you'd stop all this wishing. Oh dear, now you have me doing it.

LITTLE RABBIT. What's for supper?

MOTHER RABBIT. Cabbage soufflé.

LITTLE RABBIT. I wish you wouldn't let it burn.

MOTHER RABBIT. Burn! Do I smell something burning?

LITTLE RABBIT. I do, and it smells like cabbage soufflé.

MOTHER RABBIT (*running off*). Oh dear! My extra special dinner, and it's burning.

LITTLE RABBIT. Mother always burns everything. I wish she had a stove that wouldn't burn.

MOTHER RABBIT (*coming out*). Little Rabbit!

LITTLE RABBIT. Did you let the cabbage soufflé burn, Mother?

MOTHER RABBIT. Yes, dear. So we'll have to eat something else for supper.

LITTLE RABBIT. Good. I don't much care for souffles. I wish you'd have peppermint ice cream and cake.

MOTHER RABBIT. Stop that wishing. We're going to have lettuce turnovers. And I want you to hop next door and borrow some baking powder from Clarice Gray Squirrel.

LITTLE RABBIT. All right, Mother.

MOTHER RABBIT. Little Rabbit, go on, I need that baking powder right away. (*Goes off.*)

LITTLE RABBIT. I'm going. Hoppity hop. Oh, Mrs. Gray Squirrel.

MRS. GRAY SQUIRREL (*offstage*). Is someone calling me?

LITTLE RABBIT. I am, Mrs. Squirrel.

MRS. GRAY SQUIRREL (*offstage*). I'll be right down.

LITTLE RABBIT. I wish I lived in a tree house like the squirrels. It seems every day is housecleaning day for you, Mrs. Gray Squirrel.

MRS. GRAY SQUIRREL (*coming out*). So it is. Well, what do you want?

LITTLE RABBIT. Mother wants to borrow some baking powder.

MRS. GRAY SQUIRREL. Very well, I'll run upstairs and put some in a cup for her. (*Exits.*)

LITTLE RABBIT. I wish I had a long, bushy tail like a squirrel.

166

MRS. GRAY SQUIRREL (*returning*). Little Rabbit—

LITTLE RABBIT. Oh, back so soon, Mrs. Gray Squirrel?

MRS. GRAY SQUIRREL. I'm here—that should answer that—and I'm all out of baking powder. Sorry.

LITTLE RABBIT. Thanks just the same. I wish I had a long, bushy tail like a squirrel, and I wish I lived upstairs in a tree house, and I wish—

MRS. GRAY SQUIRREL. And I wish you'd stop all this stupid wishing, Little Rabbit, that's what I wish. Oh, for goodness' sake! You've got me wishing. Goodbye. (*Exits.*)

LITTLE RABBIT. Hoppity hop. Mother! She's out of baking powder.

MRS. RABBIT (*coming out*). Too bad. Well, it won't be long till supper. I have the lettuce turnovers on the stove now.

LITTLE RABBIT. Mother, I smell something. Something burning!

MOTHER RABBIT. Oh no, not my lettuce turnovers! Oh dear, oh dear me! (*She runs off.*)

LITTLE RABBIT. I wish Mother had a rememberer so she wouldn't forget what's cooking. Mom, I wish we had a big purple fence around the yard, with big polka dots—why is it wrong to wish?

MRS. RABBIT (*coming out again*). Little Rabbit, why don't you ask Professor Groundhog? He's one person who might explain to you why it isn't good to wish all the time.

LITTLE RABBIT. I like Professor Groundhog. Wish I had a coat like—oh, there he is! Hello, Professor Groundhog.

PROFESSOR GROUNDHOG (*entering*). Well, if it isn't my little friend Little Rabbit.

LITTLE RABBIT. It certainly is.

PROFESSOR GROUNDHOG. Yes, yes.

LITTLE RABBIT. Professor Groundhog, my mother says you're very smart and—

PROFESSOR GROUNDHOG. Yes, yes.

LITTLE RABBIT. And she says that I'm always wishing too much.

PROFESSOR GROUNDHOG. Yes, yes.

LITTLE RABBIT. And she also says that you could tell me why I shouldn't wish all the time.

PROFESSOR GROUNDHOG. Yes, yes. I mean, there is something to what your mother says, Little Rabbit. You shouldn't wish all the time. You really shouldn't.

LITTLE RABBIT. Why not? I wish you'd tell me, why not!

PROFESSOR GROUNDHOG. Well, for one thing, it makes you dissatisfied with what you have. And when you can't get what you wish for, you get upset, and are discontented, yes yes.

LITTLE RABBIT. I like to wish. I wish I had a house like yours, Professor Groundhog. You don't ever sweep the floor, do you?

PROFESSOR GROUNDHOG. I'm afraid I'm not a very good housekeeper. A bachelor schoolteacher is apt to let a house get all cluttered up. You see, there's nobody to tell me to pick up and put away.

LITTLE RABBIT. I wish nobody would tell me to pick up and put away.

PROFESSOR GROUNDHOG. Oh, I think it might be nice to have someone take care of me. Why, I even have to sew on my own buttons—

LITTLE RABBIT. Is that why your buttons don't match, Professor?

PROFESSOR GROUNDHOG. Yes, yes.

LITTLE RABBIT. I wish I had mismatched buttons.

PROFESSOR GROUNDHOG. There you go, wishing. Hmmm, if I could just make you see why you shouldn't wish so much. Hmmmm—

LITTLE RABBIT. You're a schoolteacher. You must be a very smart groundhog.

PROFESSOR GROUNDHOG. Well, there's a saying "Experience is the best teacher." And that saying may be right. Little Rabbit—

LITTLE RABBIT. Yes, Professor?

PROFESSOR GROUNDHOG. I know how you can make a wish come true.

LITTLE RABBIT. You do? You're not joking, Professor?

PROFESSOR GROUNDHOG. Yes, yes, I mean, no, no, Little Rabbit.

LITTLE RABBIT. How can I make my wish come true?

PROFESSOR GROUNDHOG. Well, deep in the forest lives an old friend of mine. He's a little elf called Pinkney Green.

LITTLE RABBIT. Can Pinkney Green make my wish come true?

PROFESSOR GROUNDHOG. He can show you a special secret wishing pond.

LITTLE RABBIT. Wishing pond! A real wishing pond?

PROFESSOR GROUNDHOG. Yes, yes. You go into the forest and find Pinkney Green, and he'll show you the magic wishing pond.

LITTLE RABBIT. And then whatever I wish will come true.

PROFESSOR GROUNDHOG. Yes, yes, and perhaps you will see how foolish it is to wish, wish, wish.

(Curtain)

Act II

SCENE. *The Wishing Pond, a tiny pool ringed with rocks and fern.*

LITTLE RABBIT. I wish I could find that elf. I wish I had an ice-cream cone. I wish—oh, is that someone behind that bush?

PINKNEY GREEN. How do you do, stranger.

LITTLE RABBIT. Oh, hi. I'm looking for—hey, you must be Pinkney Green.

PINKNEY GREEN. So I am. However did you know?

LITTLE RABBIT. You're dressed in pink and green.

PINKNEY GREEN. And why were you looking for me, might I ask?

LITTLE RABBIT. Professor Groundhog said you would show me a magic wishing pond.

PINKNEY GREEN. I don't show this wishing pond to just every Tom, Dick, and Furry who comes along.

LITTLE RABBIT. Please show it to me, Pinkney Green.

PINKNEY GREEN. Why should I?

LITTLE RABBIT. I wish all the time, and my wishes never come true.

PINKNEY GREEN. Do you make sensible wishes?

LITTLE RABBIT. Oh, yes. I wish for rocket ships and duckbills and mismatched buttons, and—

PINKNEY GREEN. Sensible wishes, umm-hmm. And what do you do to make you wishes come true, Little Rabbit?

LITTLE RABBIT. Nothing. I just wish them, and then I wish for something else.

169

PINKNEY GREEN. And just why does Professor Groundhog think I should help you?

LITTLE RABBIT. My mother sent me to him to find out just why I shouldn't wish so much, and he said, "Experience is the best teacher," and sent me here.

PINKNEY GREEN. If that's the case, I'll show you. This way.

LITTLE RABBIT. You're going to take me to the wishing pond?

PINKNEY GREEN. Here it is, among these rocks.

LITTLE RABBIT. It's very small.

PINKNEY GREEN. Its size has nothing to do with its power.

LITTLE RABBIT. Do I take a bath in it?

PINKNEY. GREEN. No, Little Rabbit, You look in the water and see your reflection; then you turn around three times; and then, the first thing you wish will come true.

LITTLE RABBIT. May I do it now?

PINKNEY GREEN. First I must warn you, Little Rabbit.

LITTLE RABBIT. Warn me?

PINKNEY GREEN. I must warn you to be sure your wish is a suitable, sensible one, for it will come true.

LITTLE RABBIT. All my wishes are good. Thanks, Pinkney Green. (*A whistle sounds. The elf disappears.*)

LITTLE RABBIT. He vanished. Oh, now I can see if the magic works. Look in the wishing pond and see my reflection—there you are, you little rabbit! I wave at you, and you wave at me. Now, turn around three times. Once, twice, and three times. And now whatever I wish will come true.

(RED BIRD *begins to fly around above* LITTLE RABBIT, *singing as he flies.*)

LITTLE RABBIT. Oh, what a pretty song! Why, it's a red bird. Stay and sing for me, Red Bird. He's flying away. Oh, what beautiful, wings, beautiful red wings. And how easily he flies through the air! Oh, I wish I had red wings.

(*Music is heard, and the red wings appear on* LITTLE RABBIT's *back.*)

LITTLE RABBIT. All of a sudden I feel so funny. My back feels heavy. Oh, what do I feel? Feathers? I did wish for red wings, didn't I?

And I have them! How grand I must look with red wings. I'm the only
little rabbit in the world with red wings.

(Curtain)

Act III

Scene. *Outside Rabbit House.*

Mrs. Rabbit. I wonder where Little Rabbit is? Here it is suppertime.
It's not like him to be late for eating. Little Rabbit!
Little Rabbit (*hopping in*). Hi, Mother.
Mrs. Rabbit. Good heavens, what's this?
Little Rabbit. What's what?
Mrs. Rabbit. This—this freak—
Little Rabbit. What freak?
Mrs. Rabbit. You!

LITTLE RABBIT. I'm not a freak, I'm your son.

MRS. RABBIT. You're no son of mine.

LITTLE RABBIT. Oh, yes, I am. Look at my red wings.

MRS. RABBIT. I am looking at them.

LITTLE RABBIT. Aren't they beautiful?

MRS. RABBIT. Beautiful! They're—they're—peculiar. Now, go away. I don't want my son to play with such a—such a monstrosity. He might wish for red wings.

LITTLE RABBIT. But I am your son, and I did wish for red wings, and my wish came true.

MRS. RABBIT. That proves you're not my son. His wishes never come true.

LITTLE RABBIT. This one did. I thought you would like my red wings.

MRS. RABBIT. You're no little rabbit of mine. Go away!

LITTLE RABBIT. I am too a rabbit. See my ears, and my fluffy tail?

MRS. RABBIT. No rabbit has red wings. Now go away.

LITTLE RABBIT. Mother, I smell something burning.

MRS. RABBIT. Burning! It must be my dandelion patties. Oh, dear, go away! (*She runs off.*)

LITTLE RABBIT. Mother, please let me in. I'm hungry. I've hopped all over the forest. Please let me in. I'm tired, and I'm hungry.

MRS. RABBIT (*offstage*). Go away, you strange thing.

LITTLE RABBIT. Mother! She won't let me in my own house. Where will I stay tonight? I can't sleep in my own bed, cause she doesn't believe I'm me. Maybe Mrs. Gray Squirrel will let me stay in her house. Mrs. Squirrel!

MRS. GRAY SQUIRREL (*offstage*). I'll be right down.

LITTLE RABBIT. She's a nice lady. I'm sure she'll let me stay here.

MRS. GRAY SQUIRREL (*coming out*). Oh! Oh, for gracious sakes, what are you?

LITTLE RABBIT. I'm a rabbit.

MRS. GRAY SQUIRREL. You can't be a rabbit. Rabbits don't have red wings.

LITTLE RABBIT. I'm Little Rabbit, and I wished for these wings.

MRS. GRAY SQUIRREL. Little Rabbit's wishes never come true. You can't be he. What do you want?

LITTLE RABBIT. I'm looking for a place to stay.

MRS. GRAY SQUIRREL. If you're Little Rabbit as you say, why don't you stay at home?

LITTLE RABBIT. My mother says I'm not her son.

MRS. GRAY SQUIRREL. She should know. Now go away, I have to wash my supper dishes.

LITTLE RABBIT. Please let me stay in your tree house, Mrs. Squirrel.

MRS. GRAY SQUIRREL. Indeed not. If I knew you, I might. But I make it a rule never to let strangers in my house.

LITTLE RABBIT. But I'm not a stranger.

MRS. GRAY SQUIRREL. Well, I don't know when I've seen anyone any stranger than you. Good-day! (*Exits.*)

LITTLE RABBIT. But Mrs. Gray Squirrel—aw, now what will I do? It's too cold to sleep outside. I wonder—Professor Groundhog! Surely he'll let me stay with him.

(Curtain)

Act IV

SCENE. *Outside the Groundhog's house. A sign on a fat tree reads:* PROFESSOR GROUNDHOG, ONE FLIGHT DOWN. *On another tree is a sign:* BROWN SQUIRRELS, TWO FLIGHTS UP.

LORELEI PUDDLEDUCK (*to* SHIRLEY SQUIRRELY). Yes, my dear, sweet Shirley Squirrely, I am so excited. The ladies of the garden club have asked me to give a talk tonight.

SHIRLEY SQUIRRELY. I know. Mother has already gone. I only wish I were old enough to belong to the Forest Ladies Garden Club.

LORELEI PUDDLEDUCK. Soon you will be. In the meanwhile, I'll give you the benefit of my vast talent. Remind me tomorrow, and I'll show you how to arrange dandelion greens in a salad bowl.

SHIRLEY SQUIRRELY. You are so kind, Lorelei. What are you going to talk about tonight?

LORELEI PUDDLEDUCK. What to do about cutworms.

SHIRLEY SQUIRRELY. What do you do about cutworms?

LORELEI PUDDLEDUCK. You eat them. They're delicious with a bit of Tabasco sauce and paprika.

SHIRLEY SQUIRRELY. I think I'd prefer a peanut butter sandwich. Well, I'll see you tomorrow. (*Exits.*)

LORELEI PUDDLEDUCK. And I'll be on my way to the meeting. (Sees LITTLE RABBIT.)

LITTLE RABBIT (*entering*). Hello, Miss Puddleduck.

LORELEI PUDDLEDUCK. What are you?

LITTLE RABBIT. I'm a rabbit. I'm Little Rabbit.

LORELEI PUDDLEDUCK. You can't be Little Rabbit. *You* have *wings!*

LITTLE RABBIT. I know.

LORELEI PUDDLEDUCK. Wings! How ridiculous!

LITTLE RABBIT. You have wings.

LORELEI PUDDLEDUCK. That's different. I am a duck. Now, stand aside, I must go.

LITTLE RABBIT. Please, Miss Puddleduck, may I stay in your house tonight?

LORELEI PUDDLEDUCK. Ohhh, of all the effrontery! Of all the nerve! Asking to stay in my house!

LITTLE RABBIT. May I?

LORELEI PUDDLEDUCK. You may not. And if you don't stop annoying me, I'll call the police dogs.

LITTLE RABBIT. Oh, don't do that!

LORELEI PUDDLEDUCK. If you're here when I return, you funny thing with wings, I'll have you put in jail. Wings, hah! (*Exits.*)

LITTLE RABBIT. Where can I stay? Oh, maybe Shirley Squirrely will let me stay in her mother's guest room. Shirley!

SHIRLEY SQUIRRELY (*entering*). Oh, hi, Little Rab—red wing. Oh, go away! (*Runs.*)

LITTLE RABBIT. Shirley, come back.

SHIRLEY SQUIRRELY (*offstage*). Mother told me never to speak to strangers, and you're strange. Go away!

LITTLE RABBIT. Nobody knows me anymore. It's getting cool, and—and I don't want to stay out all alone. Professor Groundhog—he lives one flight down. Maybe he will take pity on me. I'll go down and see. Oh, please know me, Professor, please!

(Curtain)

Act V

SCENE. *Professor Groundhog's underground house. The background is very dark. There is a flight of stairs stage right, a toadstool table with dishes of food, and a smaller toadstool for sitting, stage left.*

LITTLE RABBIT (*offstage*). Professor Groundhog! Professor!
PROFESSOR GROUNDHOG. Yes, yes, I'm coming.

LITTLE RABBIT (*barely onstage*). Professor Groundhog.

PROFESSOR GROUNDHOG. Why, it's my friend Little Rabbit.

LITTLE RABBIT. Wait till I come inside into the candlelight, then you can see my red wings.

PROFESSOR GROUNDHOG. Red wings!

LITTLE RABBIT. Yes, sir. When you see me you won't believe I'm Little Rabbit.

PROFESSOR GROUNDHOG. Nonsense. Come in, yes, yes.

LITTLE RABBIT. Thank you. (*Follows the groundhog down the steps.*)

PROFESSOR GROUNDHOG. That night air is cold and damp, bad for an individual's bones. Brings on rheumatics, arthritics, and lengthening of the hyperboles.

LITTLE RABBIT. That's why I'm here, to get out of the night air. I'd like to stay here tonight, if you'll let me.

PROFESSOR GROUNDHOG. You're always welcome here, Little Rabbit. Yes, yes. But it's late. Does your mother know you're out?

LITTLE RABBIT. She won't let me in.

PROFESSOR GROUNDHOG. Why not?

LITTLE RABBIT. Because I have red wings.

PROFESSOR GROUNDHOG. Oh yes, those red wings. Turn around. Um, hmmmm—

LITTLE RABBIT. They're real enough.

PROFESSOR GROUNDHOG. And I presume you found Pinkney Green and the wishing pond?

LITTLE RABBIT. Yes, sir, and then I saw a red bird, and his wings were so beautiful—

PROFESSOR GROUNDHOG.—That before you knew it, you wished for red wings, yes, yes.

LITTLE RABBIT. Yes, sir, and now nobody likes me, and I have no place to stay.

PROFESSOR GROUNDHOG. I suppose you could stay here tonight, Little Rabbit.

LITTLE RABBIT. Where will I sleep?

PROFESSOR GROUNDHOG. I have only one little bed, and I'm an old

groundhog—I'll have to sleep in the bed. You can find a soft spot on the floor in here.

LITTLE RABBIT. The floor doesn't look very soft.

PROFESSOR GROUNDHOG. Actually it isn't. And there are a few hickory nut shells scattered about, but it will be better than sleeping out in the dew.

LITTLE RABBIT. I'm sorta hungry, Professor Groundhog.

PROFESSOR GROUNDHOG. Luckily I had a very tasty supper, and there are some leftovers here on the table. Help yourself.

LITTLE RABBIT. What are they?

PROFESSOR GROUNDHOG. Oh, assorted delicacies: pickled worms, candied caterpillars, and snails fried in brown sugar. Just help yourself. Good-night.

LITTLE RABBIT. Good-night, Professor. Pickled worms, candied caterpillar—(*Gulps.*) I don't think I'm so hungry after all. I'll just find a cozy place on the floor to curl up and (*Jumps.*)—ow! the hickory nut shells hurt! And these wings are uncomfortable. I could be home in my own soft bed, if it weren't for these old red wings. Why did I ever wish for them?

(Curtain)

177

Act VI

SCENE. *Outside the groundhog's house.*

PROFESSOR GROUNDHOG. Good-morning, Little Rabbit.

LITTLE RABBIT (*coming outside*). Oh, is it morning? I'm glad.

PROFESSOR GROUNDHOG. Didn't you sleep well?

LITTLE RABBIT. I had a miserable night. And all on account of these ugly old red wings.

PROFESSOR GROUNDHOG. You wished for them, Little Rabbit. You have no one to blame but yourself.

LITTLE RABBIT. Is there any way to get them off?

PROFESSOR GROUNDHOG. First, we must see if experience is the best teacher.

LITTLE RABBIT. I don't know what you mean, Professor.

PROFESSOR GROUNDHOG. You got these wings just by wishing—you said the word, and there they were.

LITTLE RABBIT. Yes, sir.

PROFESSOR GROUNDHOG. You didn't take time to think, to decide whether or not that was a good wish, or what might happen if you made it. You thought of none of that. You just wished.

LITTLE RABBIT. And it was a very bad wish. Nobody likes me anymore. I can't go home—

PROFESSOR GROUNDHOG. That's why we don't get magic wishes all the time, little Rabbit. But good wishes—well, if a thing is good enough, and you work hard to make it come true, that's the only kind of wish that is worthwhile.

LITTLE RABBIT. If you work for a wish, that takes a long time.

PROFESSOR GROUNDHOG. Yes, yes, and during that time you think about whether or not it is a good thing to wish. And if it is, you will keep on working, till one day it does come true—that's the only kind of wish that is worthwhile.

LITTLE RABBIT. I think I see what you mean, Professor, but what about these old red wings?

Professor Groundhog. Lucky for you, my friend, Pinkney Green has a very special kind of wishing pond. You have learned your lesson, and so—Pinkney Green, take back your red wings! (*Music is heard and the wings disappear.*)

Little Rabbit. They're gone! I don't have those wings anymore! Oh, thank you, Professor Groundhog. From now on I'll think twice before I make wishes, and I'll never ever wish for anything foolish again.

(Curtain)

THE TWELVE MONTHS

(*A marionette play based on an old Bohemian folk tale*)

Characters

Madame Fritzelda, a large, unpleasant woman

Marushka, a very wistful, ragged little girl

Dobrunka, Madame's fat, ugly daughter, selfish and ill-tempered

Father January, a stately, elderly figure in a white robe and hood, with a white beard

Brother March, a young man in a hooded robe of light green

Brother June, not quite so young as March, in a hooded robe of bright green

Brother September, mature, in a hooded robe of apple red

The Other Eight Months, in hooded robes of appropriate color

Scrawny Cat, an optional character to be used or omitted as available time dicates.

Note. In my production Marushka sometimes has a scrawny cat. Marushka sneaks her in to get warm. Dobrunka teases and harasses the poor cat,

179

which makes the audience dislike Dobrunka all the more. She promises the cat all sorts of goodies—fish, warm cream—if the cat will lie by the stool. Dobrunka climbs up on the stool, extolling the delicious qualities of what is forthcoming, and ends up by jumping on the cat. The third time Dobrunka proposes that the cat lie beside the stool (this would take place in Act VII) the cat looks knowingly at the audience as the girl makes her promises. The cat gets in place by the stool, and, when Dobrunka counts to three before jumping, the cat springs out of the way. The girl falls in a heap on the floor, hurt and angry. Sometimes the audience applauds.

Props

Basket	Mitt, *green with a long sleeve*
Bunch of Violets	*covered to look like grass or*
Bunch of Strawberries	*leaves, worn by a puppeteer standing*
Two Apples	*by the right wing of the stage.*

The green mitt is covered during most of the production with a large piece of white cotton flannel or velveteen. The cotton looks very good but sometimes sticks to the feet of the marionettes. The white covering suggests the snow of the scene, where appropriate; on other occasions (see individual scenes where mitt is involved) the mitt is uncovered, reaches back for the flowers and fruit and puts each one in Marushka's basket. Each time when Father January regains control, the mitt covers itself with the snowy cloth.

The Other Eight Months hang on a single bar, which may be supported by hooks attached to the stage. They can be whisked on and off in a moment. They can either stand or sit. If they sit with their backs to the audience, a red light on the floor will give the effect of their fire, which will seem to grow increasingly bright as the stage lights become dimmer for the last act.

A play such as this with only two settings—but settings which keep changing—makes one wish for a revolving stage so the action could be continuous with no time out for closing curtains and waiting.

Act I

SCENE. *A peasant cottage with a fireplace (painted on the backdrop), a table, a chair, and perhaps a stool. Marushka is standing before the fire, Madame and her daughter enter.*

MADAME FRITZELDA. Marushka, what do you think you're doing?

MARUSHKA. I am warming my hands, Madame Fritzelda.

DOBRUNKA. She's taking up all the warmth from the fire. Make her move away, Mother.

MADAME FRITZELDA. Move aside, Marushka. You heard dear Dobrunka. We can't waste the good warmth of our fire on a nothing like you.

MARUSHKA. But my fingers are numb. I've been gathering firewood in the snow.

MADAME FRITZELDA. That's it, complain about your work—

DOBRUNKA. All she ever does is complain—

MADAME FRITZELDA. We brought you home with us last year out of the goodness of our hearts, and all we expect you to do is clean the house, cook the meals, mend our clothes, and milk the goat, and what do you do? Complain!

MARUSHKA. I don't mind the work, but it's so cold outside. I'd like to warm my hands, so I can milk the goat.

DOBRUNKA. Mother, I hate the way the house smells in the winter when it's all shut up so tight.

MADAME FRITZELDA. It does smell stuffy and stale.

DOBRUNKA. I like the way it smells in the spring, when we have flowers on the table.

181

MADAME FRITZELDA. What a pleasant thought, flowers—

DOBRUNKA. I want a bunch of violets for the table.

MADAME FRITZELDA. Dobrunka, it's January. There are no violets now.

DOBRUNKA. I want violets. Waaaaa, I want violets.

MADAME FRITZELDA. Mother would get you violets, if there were any to be found.

DOBRUNKA. Make Marushka get me some violets.

MADAME FRITZELDA. Marushka, you heard Dobrunka. Go fetch her some violets.

MARUSHKA. But Madame Fritzelda, there's still snow on the ground—it's the middle of winter.

DOBRUNKA. I don't care. I want violets!

MADAME FRITZELDA. And she shall have what she wants. Now go!

MARUSHKA. But the snow—it's January.

MADAME FRITZELDA. Go. And if you don't find violets, don't bother to come back at all. Now, go! (MARUSHKA *leaves.*)

(Curtain)

Act II

SCENE. *A mountainside, black and snowy.* FATHER JANUARY *stands to one side of the* OTHER EIGHT MONTHS, *who may be huddled around a fire.*

MARUAHKA (*enters, carrying her basket and not seeing the others at first*). How will I ever find violets in January? Oh, what am I going to do? Oh!

FATHER JANUARY. My child, what are you doing here on the mountainside in the snow?

MARUSHKA. How do you do, sir. I am Marushka. Madame Fritzelda sent me out for violets.

FATHER JANUARY. Does she not know that violets do not bloom until spring?

MARUSHKA. Yes. And if I do not find violets, I am not to return home.

182

FATHER JANUARY. My child, I am Father January, and these are my brothers, the Months of the Year.

MARUSHKA. Kind sir, what am I to do?

FATHER JANUARY. Brother Months, shall we help Marushka?

ALL. Yes, let's help her.

FATHER JANUARY. I will call up my brother March. Come, Brother March, you may rule long enough to help Marushka.

MARCH. What is it you wish, little girl?

MARUSHKA. Violets, if you please, March.

MARCH. Snow, melt away. Earth, become warm and green. Bring forth violets. (*Music is heard, the white snow folds back, and a green mitt uncovers itself and puts violets in* MARUSHKA's *basket.*)

MARUSHKA. Oh, what fragrant violets. Thank you, March.

MARCH. It was my pleasure.

FATHER JANUARY. Child, hurry back with your violets. Once again January must reign, with ice and snow and bitter winds. (MARUSHKA *leaves and* BROTHER MARCH *goes off, returning the reign to* FATHER JANUARY. *The mitt covers itself with the white cloth.*)

(Curtain)

Act III

SCENE. *The Cottage. The violets have been placed on the table.*

MARUSHKA. The violets do make the room smell so fresh and nice.

MADAME FRITZELDA (*entering*). Marushka! What are you doing back? What do I smell? Violets!

MARUSHKA. Yes, Madame Fritzelda. I found them on the mountainside.

MADAME FRITZELDA. Who would have believed it possible? Dobrunka!

DOBRUNKA (*entering*). Do I smell violets? Violets!

MARUSHKA. Now may I warm myself? It's very cold in the snow.

DOBRUNKA. Mother, don't let her just stand there.

MADAME FRITZELDA. Fetch some bread and jam for Dobrunka.

MARUSHKA. What kind of jam?

DOBRUNKA. Strawberry.

MARUSHKA. You ate the last of the strawberry jam last week.

DOBRUNKA. I want strawberry, waaaaa! Mother, make her get me some strawberries.

MADAME FRITZELDA. But there are no strawberries in January.

DOBRUNKA. Neither are there violets, but she found some. She can find strawberries.

MADAM FRITZELDA. Marushka, fetch some ripe strawberries for us.

MARUSHKA. But it's January—the snow.

MADAM FRITZELDA. Go! And if you don't find the strawberries, don't bother to come back at all. Now, go. (MARUSHKA *leaves.*)

(Curtain)

Act IV

SCENE. *The mountainside.* MARUSHKA *enters.*

FATHER JANUARY. What is this? Marushka, back again?

MARUSHKA. Father January, Madame Fritzelda has sent me out for ripe strawberries.

FATHER JANUARY. Strawberries! They do not ripen until June. Brother Months, shall we help Marushka again?

ALL. Yes, let's help her.

FATHER JANUARY. Brother June. Come forth, Brother June. You may rule long enough to help Marushka.

JUNE (*entering*). Little Marushka, what is it this time?

MARUSHKA. Strawberries. Ripe strawberries.

JUNE. Snow, melt away. Earth, become warm and green. Strawberries, grow and ripen for Marushka.

(*Music is heard and the mitt puts strawberries in* MARUSHKA's *basket.*)

MARUSHKA. Oh, such beautiful red strawberries. Thank you, June.

JUNE. It was my pleasure.

FATHER JANUARY. Child, hurry back with your strawberries. Once again January must reign with icy winds and freezing snow. (MARUSHKA *leaves and* BROTHER JUNE *moves aside to let* FATHER JANUARY *rule again. The mitt covers itself.*

(Curtain)

Act V

SCENE. *The cottage. The basket with the strawberries is on the table.*

MARUSHKA. I hope Dobrunka likes the strawberries.

MADAME FRITZELDA (*entering*). Marushka! How dare you come back without the straw—BERRIES! Where did you get them? (DOBRUNKA *slips in and begins to eat the berries.*)

MARUSHKA. On the mountainside. Now, please, may I warm myself by the fire?

MADAME FRITZELDA. Selfish girl! All you think about is yourself. You should be like my daughter Dobrunka, a sweet, unselfish child. Dobrunka, what are you doing?

DOBRUNKA. Noth—(*Choke*)—ing—

MADAME FRITZELDA. Have you eaten all the strawberries, without saving one for me?

DOBRUNKA. I was hungry.

MADAME FRITZELDA. Really, and I was so hungry for fresh fruit—

DOBRUNKA. We could have apples if Marushka would get them.

MADAME FRITZELDA. Apples—Marushka, fetch us some apples.

MARUSHKA. But apples do not ripen until September.

DOBRUNKA. You found violets and strawberries in the snow—you can find apples!

MADAME FRITZELDA. Go. And if you don't find apples you needn't bother to come back. The door will be locked to you. Now go!

(Quick curtain)

Act VI

SCENE. *The mountainside.* MARUSHKA *enters with basket.*

FATHER JANUARY. Marushka, it grows late. Why are you here on the mountainside?

MARUSHKA. This time I must have apples.

FATHER JANUARY. Apples? They ripen during the time of September. Brother Months, shall we help Marushka again?

ALL. Yes, we will help her.

FATHER JANUARY. Brother September, come forth and rule for a while.

SEPTEMBER. What is your wish, Marushka?

MARUSHKA. Apples, if you please, sir.

SEPTEMBER. Snow, melt away. Earth, become warm and green. Trees, bear fruit—apples red and gold for Marushka. (*Music; the mitt puts two apples in the basket.*)

MARUSHKA. Apples! Oh, thank, you, September.

SEPTEMBER. Now I must take my place by the fire. (*Exits.*)

FATHER JANUARY. Child, hurry home with your apples, for once again January must reign with fingers of ice and drifts of snow that bring chills—and cold! (MARUSHKA *leaves. Mitt covers itself in snowy cloth.*)

(Curtain)

186

Act VII

SCENE. *The cottage.*

MARUSHKA. (*entering*). Dobrunka, I have two apples here.

DOBRUNKA. Only two? Why didn't you bring more?

MARUSHKA. That's all I could find, only two.

DOBRUNKA. Any apple tree bears more than two apples. I'll find that tree and fill my apron with apples. I'm going!

MARUSHKA. No, Dobrunka, you'll never find it! (DOBRUNKA *runs out.*)

MADAME FRITZELDA (*entering*). Where is Dobrunka?

MARUSHKA. She has gone to find an apple tree that isn't there.

MADAME FRITZELDA. Why did you let her go? It's almost dark! She'll lose her way in the snow. I must catch her! Dobrunka! (*She runs out, crying.*) Dobrunka!

MARUSHKA. I must stop both of them. Madame Fritzelda! Dobrunka! (*She runs off.*)

(Curtain)

Act VIII

SCENE. *The mountainside.*

DOBRUNKA (*entering*). I'll find that apple tree, and I'll eat all the apples I please, and then I'll fill my apron and—oh! Who are you? Where's the apple tree, old man?

FATHER JANUARY. What apple tree, my child?

DOBRUNKA. I don't know. You tell me where it is or I'll kick you. There. (*She kicks him in the shins and starts off behind the group of Eight Months.*)

FATHER JANUARY. Oh, child, come back. Don't go up the mountain. Stop!

DOBRUNKA. I'll go where I please, you stupid old man. (*Runs off.*)

FATHER JANUARY. Poor, stubborn girl.

MADAME FRITZELDA (*running onstage*). Dobrunka! Dobrunka! Old man, have you seen my daughter?

FATHER JANUARY. A girl passed this way—but you must not follow her.

MADAME FRITZELDA. Out of my way, you old—(*Pushes him aside.*) Dobrunka! (*Runs off stage.*)

FATHER JANUARY. Do not try to follow her, Madame. You will never come back. It is too late!

MARUSHKA (*rushing onstage*). Father January!

FATHER JANUARY. Marushka, my child.

MARUSHKA. Father January, have you seen Dobrunka and Madame Fritzelda?

FATHER JANUARY. Were they the ones who sent you out into the snow?

MARUSHKA. Yes, but we must save them. Do you know where they are?

FATHER JANUARY. Yes, and it is too late for anyone to help them. I tried to stop them.

MARUSHKA. Where have they gone?

FATHER JANUARY. Up this mountain. They are now nothing but snow at the top of the mountain. There they will remain the year round—snow, never melting, no matter the season.

MARUSHKA. Oh, Father January, what is to become of me?

FATHER JANUARY. You will return to the cottage, for it now belongs to you. And there you will live happily, for the twelve months will smile down on you for the rest of your life.

(Curtain)

THE PLUMP PRINCESS

(An original fairy tale for marionettes)

Characters

QUEEN. An elegant lady, somewhat put out about having an unattractive daughter

KING IGNATIUS, a large chap, a bit more folksy than his wife. (No doubt the princess inherits her plumpness from him.)

PRINCESS FRUMPTIOUS, large and possibly pretty beneath all the fat. She is very nicely coiffed and dressed, but all this is obscured in the beginning by a stringy wig that covers her hair and a crumpled apron that covers her skirt, its sashes trailing on the floor behind her.

CUMQUAT, a tall, likable servant wearing an apron with the royal crest.

ELF, a cheerful little fellow with feather hair

ELF KING, the neatest, chubbiest little king you have ever seen, with a feather beard

SERVANT, another elf

JUNE BUG, a huge, busy, buzzy bug

Props

The princess' breakfast tray should be attached to the table. It can be covered either by a cloth or a pseudo silver lid, with a string so Cumquat can remove it.

The Elf King's breakfast should be colorful, with unusual dishes to contrast with the realistic quality of the other castle.

Act I

SCENE. *Castle room. Royal trappings on backdrop. A table and stool are the only necessary pieces of furniture.*

QUEEN. Princess Frumptious, I do wish you'd hurry. Your breakfast is getting cold.

PRINCESS *offstage*). I'm coming. (*Enters.*)

QUEEN. Good morning, Princess. Look at you. You're a perfect fright. Really, I've never seen a girl like you.

PRINCESS. I can't help it if I'm fat.

QUEEN. Go back and comb your hair, do you hear? Honestly, it looks like a haystack.

PRINCESS (*as she exits*). You wouldn't say that if I weren't fat.

QUEEN. Ignatius!

KING IGNATIUS (*entering*). What is it, my dear? I'm very busy, you know.

QUEEN. I know that, my dear King, but this is important. It's about our daughter Frumptious.

KING IGNATIUS. What has Frumpy done now?

QUEEN. Frumpy! You called our daughter Frumpy!

KING IGNATIUS. Why not? Everyone else does.

QUEEN. Not really!

KING IGNATIUS. Perhaps not where you can hear them, my dear, but Frumpy she's called by almost everyone.

QUEEN. Do you know what Frumpy means?

KING IGNATIUS. I have a vague idea.

QUEEN. It means dowdy and lazy—

KING IGNATIUS. That's our Frumpy.

QUEEN. I wish you wouldn't call her that. It's unpleasant.

KING IGNATIUS. No one would call her that if she weren't so dowdy and lazy. She never combs her hair, and her ribbons and sashes are always untied and dragging along the floor. She is a most unseemly princess. In fact, she's not like a princess at all.

190

QUEEN. And that's what I want to discuss with you, Ignatius. What can we do about Frumptious?

KING IGNATIUS. I could issue a proclamation that all princesses must henceforth be neat and tidy and mannerly.

QUEEN. A lot of good that would do. Frumptious is too lazy to read a proclamation.

KING IGNATIUS. We could send her away to finishing school.

QUEEN. And she would disgrace us. Would you want everyone outside the palace to know that the Princess is so—so—

KING IGNATIUS. Frumpy?

QUEEN. Exactly. Would you want them to think that we have failed as parents, with such a daughter?

KING IGNATIUS. Indeed I wouldn't, now that you put it that way.

QUEEN. Then exactly what can we do, Ignatious?

KING IGNATIUS. I'll put my head to thinking. I have so many things to do, and remember, my dear, the Duke's daughter will be here to lunch with the Princess.

QUEEN. Not today!

KING IGNATIUS. Today. Good impression very important, my dear, very. The Duke is very sensitive. If Frumpy—er, Frumptious—if she were to insult the Duke's daughter, he might challenge me to a duel. And he's very good with a sword.

QUEEN. Oh dear! And I have an appointment in town to shop with the Countess—

KING IGNATIUS. I must be running along, my dear. The Royal Ministers are waiting for my Royal Presence in the Royal Council Room. (*Exits.*)

QUEEN. Before I leave, I must get Frumptious to improve her eating manners. She really knows better than she acts, it's just that she doesn't care. Frumptious! Your breakfast is getting colder and colder. I must talk with her.

CUMQUAT. Begging your pardon, Your Majesty—

QUEEN. Yes, what is it, Cumquat?

CUMQUAT. Has the Princess Frumpy—

QUEEN. Cumquat!

CUMQUAT. Ulp! I beg your pardon—er, has the Princess Frumptious had her breakfast?

QUEEN. Not yet. Her breakfast must be cold and tasteless by now.

CUMQUAT. Oh, I think not, Your Majesty. I used the special dishes that keep it warm. You know the Princess is always late for her meals.

QUEEN. Sad but true. Frumptious!

PRINCESS (*offstage*). I'm coming.

QUEEN. Cumquat, you may uncover her breakfast tray.

CUMQUAT. With pleasure. (*Uncovers tray.*)

QUEEN. Oh, how delicious it looks. Cumquat, I must say that you servants are very nice to the Princess—although she hardly deserves it.

CUMQUAT. We try to please her. It would mean so much if she would say just one nice thing about the food so I could tell the Royal Cook. Every day he asks me if the Princess has anything to say about his cooking, but never a word does she say.

QUEEN. Something must be done. Frumptious!

PRINCESS. I'm hungry, where's breakfast?

QUEEN. It's on the table where it usually is.

CUMQUAT. Good morning, Princess.

(*The* PRINCESS *yawns.*)

CUMQUAT. Good morning, Princess.

PRINCESS. Slurp—

QUEEN. Frumptious, aren't you going to speak to Cumquat? After all, he did bring you this lovely breakfast.

(THE PRINCESS *chews noisily, chomp, chomp.*)

CUMQUAT. Cook prepared the special butterscotch waffles that you like so much, Your Highness.

THE PRINCESS. *Glub, chomp, slurp—*

QUEEN. Listen to you! Is that any way for a royal princess to eat? Why, the pigs in the barnyard make less noise. Aren't you ashamed?

PRINCESS. You wouldn't call me a pig if I weren't so fat.

QUEEN. Do try to eat like a lady. After all, you've had the best teachers—

PRINCESS. I don't ca—chomp!

QUEEN. Don't try to talk when your mouth is full, Frumptious.

PRINCESS. You're always picking on—slurp, chomp, glub—

QUEEN. Oh, this is too much! I can't stand another minute of this! (*Exits.*) I'll be late for my appointment with the Countess. Why did I have to have a daughter like this? Why?

PRINCESS. She's always making fun of me because I'm fat.

CUMQUAT. Princess, if I might make a suggestion—your mother would be so pleased if you try to eat a bit more quietly. You know, not so much slurp, slurp and chomp, chomp.

PRINCESS. You don't like me either.

CUMQUAT. Oh, but I do, Frumpy, I mean Princess.

PRINCESS. No, you don't. You're just like everybody else. Get out!

CUMQUAT. But Frumpy!

PRINCESS. Everybody calls me Frumpy, and I don't like it! Now, get out and leave me alone.

CUMQUAT. Yes, Your Highness. (*Exits.*)

PRINCESS. Just because I'm fat, they make fun of me. They fuss at me. I never do anything right. Oh (*sob*), I hate everybody. Boo-hoooo—and all because I'm fat.

ELF (*popping in*). What's going on here?

PRINCESS. Go away.

ELF. You tell me to go away, but you don't even know who I am.

PRINCESS. I don't care. Go away and leave me alone. You won't like me either because I'm fat.

ELF. Oh, I like most fat people.

PRINCESS. You do?

ELF. Most of the time. Now, dry your eyes—

PRINCESS. Where are you?

ELF. Down here.

PRINCESS. Oh, who are you?

ELF. I'm an elf. And you must be Princess Frumptious.

PRINCESS. Everybody calls me Frumpy—everybody except my mother—and she thinks I'm frumpy, the same as everybody.

ELF. Maybe they just don't like tangled hair and untied ribbons.

PRINCESS. They just don't like me because I'm fat. They think I'm ugly and fat, fat, fat!

ELF. Now, hold on, Princess. I think you're in need of a little visit.

PRINCESS. I don't want to go visiting. Nobody likes me when I go visiting.

ELF. You've never been to a place like I want to take you to, down into Elf Land.

PRINCESS. Elf Land. Oh, you elves are so tiny. Your friends won't like me, because I'm so big and fat.

ELF. No, no, no, Princess. I know someone who is very fat, and everybody likes him. They like him very much.

PRINCESS. Do they really?

ELF. There's no doubt about it. Now you just follow me, and we're off for Elf Land!

(Curtain)

Act II

SCENE. *Elf Land Throne Room. The room should be very imaginative and sparkly, with vines or large flowers entwining to make the elves look smaller. Should include the throne and a table and chair.*

ELF. Right this way, Princess.

PRINCESS. Oh, what a lovely little—it looks like a little throne room.

ELF. And that's exactly what it is. This is where the Elf King stays.

PRINCESS. Elf King?

ELF. Wait till you see him. But now I think it would be best if we hid over here.

PRINCESS. Would I frighten him away because I'm so fat?

ELF. No, no, Princess. It's just that I want you to see him before you meet him.

PRINCESS. Whatever you think is best.

ELF. Why, Princess. Already you're being agreeable.

PRINCESS. I'll be very quiet. (*They hide.*)

SERVANT (*entering*). Oh, it's time for the Elf King's breakfast. He was up so late last night giving prizes at the Fairyland Ball that we let him sleep later than usual. Ah, the breakfast is here, and it's piping hot. Oh, good morning, Your Majesty.

ELF KING (*entering*). Good morning, dear friend. Is that a new jacket you're wearing? Very handsome.

SERVANT. It should be, Sire. It's the one you gave me for my birthday last week.

ELF KING. Ho, ho, so it is. Would you look me over, I'm so roly-poly that I can't see all around myself, even in my mirrors, ho, ho.

SERVANT. Oh, there's a little wrinkle in your royal robe. There now, it's gone.

ELF KING. I must look my best. You see, everyone wants to look up to his king, and therefore the king should be worthy.

SERVANT. Your Majesty never, never looks frumpy. Never.

ELF KING. It's kind of you to say so. Do I smell breakfast?

SERVANT. Indeed you do. Look.

ELF KING. A breakfast fit for a king, ho, ho. And—oh, never did I taste such delicious muffins. Here, taste this—

SERVANT. Oh, it is delicious.

ELF KING. You must tell the cook that—no, I'll tell him myself. And this peppermint tea! I will have a new medal made to pin on the cook's apron.

SERVANT. When Your Majesty appreciates everything so much, well, everyone tries all the more to do his best. You're the very best Elf King we've ever had.

ELF KING. Oh, come now, you must not flatter me too much. Listen, do you hear that buzzing?

SERVANT. It sounds like that June Bug is coming back again.

(JUNE BUG *flies through, causing a great commotion.*)

ELF KING. And he's tangled up in my morning-glory vine.

SERVANT. Go away, you ugly bug. Go away!

ELF KING. It's no good yelling at him.

SERVANT. You command him to stay away from Elf Palace. He has plenty of places to fly without bothering us.

ELF KING. No, no. I will try to make him understand that we can't allow June bugs to fly in. Otherwise, all the horseflies and bumblebees and wasps would insist on buzzing in and out, and we could never allow that. I will speak firmly to him, and take him a bit of bread and jam. (*Exits.*)

SERVANT. What a kind person the Elf King is, even when he has to scold, he takes along a bit of bread and jam. Well, I can't stand here all day. There's too much to be done. (*Exits and calls back from offstage.*) I must press His Majesty's afternoon suit. He is so neat.

(ELF *and* PRINCESS *come out.*)

ELF. Now, Princess Frumptious, did you ever see anyone roly-er and poly-er than the Elf King?

PRINCESS. He is rather plump.

ELF. He is more than plump. I would say that he is downright fat.

PRINCESS. Yes, he is. But he is so nice. And looks so nice in his clothes. I didn't think a fat person could look that way.

Act II

SCENE. *Princess' Castle. Should be very elegant.*

(NOGARD *and* BUNNY *fly in.*)

NOGARD. We're landing, Bunny. Easy does it—

BUNNY. Oh, that was fun. No time at all, and here we are in a castle.

NOGARD. And here comes a little princess. I'll hide.

BUNNY. What shall I say?

NOGARD. "How-do-you-do" is a nice beginning.

PRINCESS (*entering*). Oh, hello.

BUNNY. How-do-you-do. I'm Bunny.

ELF. Certainly a fat person can look nice—if he, or she, is neat. The King's shoes are always tied, and his hair neatly combed.

PRINCESS. I wish I could be like the Elf King. Then everybody would like me. (JUNE BUG *flies through.*)

ELF. He's coming in. Princess, are you ready to meet him?

PRINCESS. Oh, no. He won't like me, because I'm fat.

ELF. But he's fat too. Now, remember your manners. Oh, Your Majesty!

ELF KING (*entering*). Good morning, dear friend, you look quite chipper this morning.

ELF. And so do you. How did you get rid of the June Bug?

ELF KING. I persuaded him to fly over across the meadow. I heard there was a June bug picnic taking place today. Oh, oh, who is this? My dear, forgive me. I was very rude not to speak sooner, but my mind was on that June Bug.

PRINCESS. Oh, that's quite all right, Your Majesty. I know how it is with kings. My father always has something more important on his mind.

ELF KING. My, my, aren't you a pretty child!

PRINCESS. No one ever called me pretty before.

ELF KING. And such pretty golden hair. You know, every fairy-tale princess has golden hair, so you can be a real fairy-tale princess.

PRINCESS. No, no I can't.

ELF KING. And why not?

PRINCESS. Everybody says that I'm not like a princess at all.

ELF. She thinks no one likes her—

PRINCESS. Because I'm fat.

ELF KING. Nonsense. That's no reason. Hmmm—maybe you need a magic charm.

PRINCESS. A magic charm to make people like me?

ELF KING. You might call it that.

ELF. I would suggest you borrow his magic charm, Princess Frumptious.

PRINCESS. Please, Your Majesty, will you give it to me?

ELF KING. Of course, of course. Come here, and I will whisper it in your ear.

PRINCESS. Oh, can't I see it?

ELF KING. No, but if you use it, everybody else will see it. Now, listen carefully. (KING *whispers to* FRUMPTIOUS.)

PRINCESS. Oh—oh—you think it will make people like me, even if I am fat?

ELF KING. I'm sure of it.

ELF. Now, Princess, we had better take you back home before it gets any later.

PRINCESS. That's right I'm having guests to lunch. Thank you so much, Your Majesty.

ELF KING. Don't mention it, my dear. Good-bye.

PRINCESS. Good-bye.

ELF. Follow me, Princess. Hurry!

(Curtain)

Act III

SCENE. *Castle room.*

QUEEN. Where's the Princess? Where is she?

KING IGNATIUS. My dear, I thought you had gone to town with the countess.

QUEEN. I started, but I just had to come back. I couldn't enjoy myself for thinking about the Princess and the Duke's daughter.

KING INGNATIUS. I know what you mean. Frumpy, er, Frumptious will probably look so frumpy—and act so frumpy—that the Duke's daughter will be insulted.

QUEEN. Where is the girl? Frumptious!

KING. Come to think of it, I haven't seen her for an hour or more.

QUEEN. I must give her instructions. She eats like a little pig. And her hair is never combed, and her sashes—Frumptious!

KING IGNATIUS. Shall I call out the guards to search for her?

QUEEN. Oh, this is dreadful. Frumptious!

PRINCESS (*running in*). Oh, hello. Did you call?

QUEEN. Did we call? I've been bellowing like a fishwife.

PRINCESS. I'm sorry. But you must excuse me now. I have so much to do, and there's so little time. (*Exits.*) Excuse me, please, dear Mama.

QUEEN. Certainly, dear, certainly. What am I saying? She spoke so sweetly and politely that I forgot what I was doing.

KING IGNATIUS. I've never known Frumpy to be so mannerly.

QUEEN. Frumptious, we must speak to you before lunchtime.

PRINCESS (*offstage*). In just a minute, dear Mama. I will hurry.

QUEEN. That's a sweet girl. I must think of some way to get her sashes tied and her hair brushed—

KING IGNATIUS. Maybe you could promise her a new dress, or a trip to the park to ride on the merry-go-round, or—

PRINCESS (*entering with her hair neat and her sashes tied*). Now, what is it, Mama dear?

QUEEN. Frumptious! Look at you. Your hair is combed.

199

KING IGNATIUS. I had no idea your hair was so curly.

QUEEN. And your sashes are tied so neatly!

PRINCESS. And my shoestrings, too.

QUEEN. I must say it's quite an improvement.

PRINCESS. Thank you.

KING IGNATIUS. And you're actually acting like a princess.

QUEEN. Really, Ignatius, our daughter isn't nearly as horrible looking as I have thought.

KING IGNATIUS. Frumptious, dear, the Duke's daughter will be here for lunch, and—

QUEEN. And as you know, the Duke is a very touchy person. If he thinks you don't like his daughter—

PRINCESS. Oh, but she's such a nice little girl. I'll do my best to entertain her.

KING IGNATIUS. And if you are disagreeable with her, she'll tell her father and he'll challenge me to a duel, and—did you say you would be nice to her?

PRINCESS. Certainly. I'll even show her all my dolls and we can walk in the prettiest part of the garden—

QUEEN. Oh, this is too good to be true. Ignatius, what has happened to our daughter?

KING IGNATIUS. I don't know, but it's certainly a change for the better.

QUEEN. Frumptious, could you tell us what, er, that is—

PRINCESS. Certainly I'll tell you. I visited the King of Elf Land, and he gave me a secret charm.

QUEEN. A secret charm?

PRINCESS. Yes, it's a secret, but I'm sure he won't mind if I tell you. He told me that if I would be neat, everyone would think I'm sweet; and that if I try to be nice, no one would care if I'm very fat.

QUEEN. Oh, that's a wonderful secret charm.

PRINCESS. But don't tell anyone.

KING IGNATIUS. Certainly not. They will see for themselves. This charm has made you charming, Frumptious.

PRINCESS. Now, if you'll excuse me again, I must speak to the royal cook. I'm sure if I ask him nicely he'll make some special little chocolate cupcakes for the Duke's daughter. (*Exits.*)

QUEEN. Well, in all her life she has never been so, so—well, so nice.

KING IGNATIUS. If she keeps this up, no one will ever call her Frumpy again.

QUEEN. Oh, but they're bound to, with a name like Frumptious. Why did we ever give her such a name?

KING IGNATIUS. Don't you remember? She was named for my great aunt. You know, that disagreeable old lady.

QUEEN. Well, I must say I'm sorry we gave our dear, sweet daughter such an ugly name.

KING IGNATIUS. My dear, I'm not the King for nothing. I will send for the Keeper of the Royal Records, and we'll change her name.

QUEEN. Change Frumptious' name?

KING IGNATIUS. Yes, indeed. Instead of calling her Frumptious, now everyone shall call her Scrumptious.

QUEEN. Scrumptious! What a scrumptious name.

KING IGNATIUS. A scrumptious name for a scrumptious princess—a plump princess—whom everyone will like.

(Curtain)

201

STAY-HOME BUNNY

(*An original marionette play for younger children*)

Characters

BUNNY, a preschool bunny in a nightgown

MOTHER, all dressed up in hat and coat

MRS. FIELDMOUSE (Wouldn't you know Felicia would turn up sooner or later!)

NOGARD DRAGON, a friendly dragon of the type with wings

PRINCESS, a little girl, very pretty and regal, wearing a crown

KING, also regal, in traditional crown and robe

SKUNK, not unpleasant

BIG BAD WOLF, not pleasant!

Act I

SCENE. BUNNY's *bedroom. Must contain cradle, may have other nursery equipment or furnishings as desired.*

MOTHER. Bunny, Mother is going out tonight.

BUNNY. I want to go too, Mummy.

MOTHER. I'm sorry, dear, but I'm going to a meeting of the garden club, and little bunnies cannot go.

BUNNY. Please, may I go?

MOTHER. No, Bunny, you must stay home.

BUNNY. Stay home—that's all I ever do.

MOTHER. Soon Mrs. Fieldmouse will be here to baby-sit with you, and then I must go.

BUNNY. I don't want to stay home.

MOTHER. You be a sweet bunny with Mrs. Fieldmouse.

(*A knock is heard at the door.*)

BUNNY. Somebody's at the door.

MOTHER. I'll see—oh, Mrs. Fieldmouse, do come right in.

MRS. FIELDMOUSE (*entering*). I hope I'm not late.

MOTHER. No, no, but it is time for me to leave. I don't want to be late for the garden club meeting. Lorelei Puddleduck is going to show how to arrange fern fronds in a frozen-orange-juice can.

MRS. FIELDMOUSE. I'm not a fancy flower arranger myself. Just give me a pot of red geraniums and I'm happy.

MOTHER. I set out the cocoa and the pecans in case you decide to make some nutty fudge tonight. And I'll be back early. Bunny, you be a good girl, and mind Mrs. Fieldmouse.

BUNNY. Why do I have to stay home?

MOTHER. No more of that.

BUNNY. If you don't let me go, I'll throw a tantrum.

MOTHER. It won't do you a bit of good.

BUNNY. I'll scream and kick and cry, and then you'll let me go.

MOTHER. Bunny, you can throw three tantrums and then three more, and I won't watch. I'm leaving now. See you later, Mrs. Fieldmouse. (*Leaves.*)

MRS. FIELDMOUSE. Enjoy the meeting, my dear. Goodbye. Now, Bunny, here we are.

BUNNY. I'm going to throw my tantrum.

MRS. FIELDMOUSE. That's nice.

BUNNY. Don't you care?

MRS. FIELDMOUSE. If throwing a tantrum will make you feel better, throw one. I don't mind. Heavens, I've seen many a tantrum in my day. In fact, I'll bet I can kick harder and cry louder than you.

BUNNY. Grown people aren't supposed to throw tantrums.

MRS. FIELDMOUSE. Neither are children, but if you want to be naughty, I'll be naughty too. Watch. Waaaa, Waaaa! I'm mad. I don't wanna do this! (*Jumps up and down.*) I don't wanna do that, waaaaaa—Are you watching, Bunny?

BUNNY. You're silly.

MRS. FIELDMOUSE. Now, I've had my tantrum. Are you going to have yours?

BUNNY. No.

MRS. FIELDMOUSE. Why not?

BUNNY. It's no fun to have it, if you want me to have it.

MRS. FIELDMOUSE. Oh, pity, pity. Your mother said I could make some fudge—

BUNNY. Mrs. Fieldmouse, why do I always have to stay home?

MRS. FIELDMOUSE. Because you are a little bunny. When you're bigger you can do as you please. Now, jump into bed, dear.

BUNNY. Somebody always tells me what to do. I wish nobody would say, "Do this," or "Do that."

MRS. FIELDMOUSE. Would you like some nutty fudge?

BUNNY. Maybe. Mrs. Fieldmouse, do you believe in dragons?

MRS. FIELDMOUSE. Do I believe in dragons?

BUNNY. Well, do you?

MRS. FIELDMOUSE. I can't say that I ever saw one—

BUNNY. I have a dragon friend. His name is Nogard. That's dragon spelled backwards.

MRS. FIELDMOUSE. That's nice.

BUNNY. He comes to play with me sometimes, specially when I have to stay home.

MRS. FIELDMOUSE. That's nice. I think I'll go out to the kitchen and make some fudge—(*She goes off.*)

BUNNY. She doesn't believe I know a dragon at all. But I do. I hope he'll come to see me tonight. Nogard! Nogard!

MRS. FIELDMOUSE (*offstage*). Are you calling me, Bunny?

BUNNY. No, I'm calling my dragon.

MRS. FIELDMOUSE (*offstage*). That's nice.

BUNNY. Nogard, please come to talk with me.

NOGARD (*flying in*). Zoooom—hello there, Bunny.

BUNNY. Oh, Nogard! You've come to see me.

NOGARD. It's time for beddie-bye. That's why I'm here.

BUNNY. Nogard, why do I always have to be a stay-home Bunny? And don't say it's because I'm little.

NOGARD. That's exactly what I was going to say. How did you know?

BUNNY. Oh, that's what everybody tells me. I want to go somewhere, and do things.

NOGARD. Anyplace in particular?

BUNNY. I dunno. Oh, yes, I do. I'd like to visit a princess. Princesses must have fun all the time—they can do just as they please. Could I visit a princess, Nogard?

NOGARD Hmmmm, I suppose. We'll fly?

BUNNY. You have wings, but how can I fly?

NOGARD. Just touch my wing, and you can fly, too.

BUNNY. Like this? (*She touches his wing.*)

NOGARD. Like that. Now, shall we fly?

BUNNY. Let's! (*They fly around.*) Oh, I'm flying!

NOGARD. No trick at all when you're imaginary. Now, this way to visit a princess. (*They fly off.*)

(Curtain)

PRINCESS. I am the Princess, and I suppose I do very well.

BUNNY. This is a lovely castle.

PRINCESS. But I get so tired of staying in it all the time.

BUNNY. Oh, I wouldn't ever get tired of staying in a place this beautiful. When we were flying over—oh, you haven't met Nogard, my dragon.

PRINCESS. A dragon? Where?

BUNNY. Over there. You can't see him unless you imagine real hard.

PRINCESS. Oh, I can imagine as hard as anyone. Oh, I see him. Hello, Dragon.

NOGARD. Turn that around backwards and you'll have my name.

PRINCESS. Dragon—Nogard. Oh, I see. Bunny, I never have any fun like this.

BUNNY. As I was saying, when we were flying over, I saw the nicest little brook, just like the one at home. Do you ever go wading in the brook?

PRINCESS. Oh, no! Father wouldn't let me. He says a princess should be dignified.

BUNNY. Dignified, what's that?

NOGARD. It's what grown-ups try to be. You know: "Ahem, mind your manners"; "Stand up straight"; "Ahem, ahem"—

BUNNY. Like my uncle Ravenscroft Rabbit.

PRINCESS. Oh, my father is coming—

NOGARD. Shall I hide?

PRINCESS. You needn't bother, Nogard. Father has no imagination at all. But, Bunny, you had better stay out of sight.

BUNNY. Why?

(BUNNY *leaves just as the princess speaks.*)

PRINCESS. I'm not allowed to have visitors except on visitors' day. Hello, Father.

KING (*enters.*) My dear Princess. I'm afraid we cannot go riding this afternoon.

PRINCESS. But you promised!

KING. I know, but the Prime Minister and the Keeper of the Exchequer are coming for a conference.

PRINCESS. You're the king, Father. Tell them you can't have a conference, that you're going riding.

KING. It's not that simple, my dear. I may be the king, but still have to do as I am told. Now they're waiting for me. I'm terribly sorry.

PRINCESS. So am I. (*The* KING *leaves.*)

BUNNY. Can't the King ride when he pleases?

PRINCESS. No. It's always like this. None of us can do as we please.

BUNNY. Nogard, I thought a princess always did as she pleased.

NOGARD. It seems she doesn't. Are you ready to go home?

BUNNY. If I go home, I'll have to keep on doing what I'm told. Let's go somewhere, Nogard, where no one ever tells anybody what to do. Is there such a place?

NOGARD. I just happen to know of such a place. It's called Wild, Wild Woods.

BUNNY. Please take me.

NOGARD. Touch my wing. (*Up they go.*)

BUNNY. We're flying! Good-bye, Princess.

PRINCESS. Good-bye, Bunny. Good-bye, Dragon.

NOGARD. To the Wild, Wild Woods! (*They fly off.*)

(Curtain)

Act III

SCENE. *The Wild, Wild Woods: The backdrop is thick with trees. A tree stump big enough for* BUNNY *to hide in stands a bit left of center stage.*

(NOGARD *and* BUNNY *fly in.*)

NOGARD. Down we go!

BUNNY. Oh, I don't think I like this place. Where are the paths?

NOGARD. No one tells anyone to keep the paths neat, so there are no paths.

BUNNY. It's almost dinnertime. I hope someone will invite us to dinner.

NOGARD. Bunny, I know this is the Wild, Wild Woods, and no one

ever tells anyone else what to do, but if I might make a suggestion—hide in the bushes! Someone is coming, and in this place you never know if a person is friendly or fierce. (*Exits.*)

SKUNK (*entering*). Oh, de-doe-de-doe, traddle-de-dah—

BUNNY. A skunk!

SKUNK. Did someone say something? Oh, hello.

BUNNY. Hello, I'm Bunny.

SKUNK. So you are. My-oh-my, I'm hungry.

BUNNY. I am, too.

SKUNK. I would invite you home to dinner, but nobody told me to stay home, so I left. And here I am.

BUNNY. Aren't you going to eat dinner somewhere?

SKUNK. If I can find something. You see, no one ever tells me to help with dinner, so I never have any dinner.

BUNNY. My mother always says, "Bunny, set the table and we'll have dinner."

WOLF (*offstage*). Gr-r-r-r-r!

BUNNY. What was that?

SKUNK. It's a most ferocious wolf! I'm going to hide.

BUNNY. Why?

SKUNK. He eats all the animals that are smaller than himself. I won't tell you what to do, but I'm—(*Dashes off.*)

WOLF. I smell rabbit! Tender, young rabbit, gr-r-r-r-r!

BUNNY. Oh, dear, I had better hide. Maybe he won't see me in this hollow tree stump. In I jump—

WOLF (*looking around*). I'm sure I smell rabbit! Is there a rabbit around here? In this hollow tree stump? (BUNNY *jumps out before he looks in.*) No, not in there. I was sure I smelled rabbit. I know. On the other side! *Bends down to look and* BUNNY *jumps back in.*) Not there. Maybe the rabbit is deeper in the woods, gr-r-r-——(*Goes off.*)

NOGARD (*coming out*). Bunny, are you safe?

BUNNY. I think so—except I'm half scared to death. Nogard, I'm hungry.

NOGARD. Don't you like it here in the woods where no one tells you what to do?

BUNNY. No. I don't like it at all. If we were any other place, I'd tell you to take me home. Here I can only ask you, but please take me home. Please take me home.

NOGARD. Asking is much nicer. Touch my wing—and we're flying! (*They fly off.*)

(Curtain)

Act IV

SCENE. BUNNY'*s bedroom.*

NOGARD (*flying in with* BUNNY). Back into your cradle, Bunny.

BUNNY. It's so good to be home again.

NOGARD. And, if you don't mind, it's my bedtime too. I'll be "dragoning" along.

BUNNY. Thank you for the trip, Nogard. Good-night!

NOGARD. Good-night! (*Flies off.*)

MRS. FIELDMOUSE (*coming in*). La-da-da, Bunny, the fudge is almost hard enough to cut—oh, is she asleep?

MOTHER (*entering*). Mrs. Fieldmouse! I'm back!

MRS. FIELDMOUSE. Oh, I didn't expect you this early.

MOTHER. The meeting was over sooner than I expected. Bunny—oh, she's asleep.

BUNNY. No, I'm not, Mummy.

MOTHER. Bunny, I hurried home. I thought how you always have to stay home, so I said to myself, "We can take a little walk in the woods, down by the nollow tree stump"—if you want to, Bunny.

BUNNY. Some other time, maybe, Mummy. But for now, guess what?

MOTHER. What, dear?

BUNNY. I want to stay home.

(Curtain)

V

PUPPETS IN OTHER PLACES

IN THE CLASSROOM

Puppetry offers a wide scope of activities for the classroom. It can start as an experience in arts and crafts, with the making of the puppets. The class can write an original play or adapt a favorite story, a pleasant exercise in English; or foreign words can be introduced as part of language study. The subject matter can be taken from geography and history, from current events, or social problems. Designing and building the stage will give students with a mechanical bent a chance to shine. The performance will tie all the many facets together with drama. The project can be as simple as a first-grade reader or as complicated as a tenth-grade Latin book.

Working with puppets can ease tensions, release inhibitions, in a constructive way. A shy child can blossom as a wit and a wonder—when only his puppet is seen. Puppetry is great therapy, there's no doubt about that.

I had my first taste of puppetry in junior high when the art class decided to make marionettes. The art teacher, who was also the English teacher, went to the library and found a book on marionettes* with an outline for *The Childhood of David Copperfield.* We made heads of paper-mache in the old-fashioned way with shredded newspaper and paste, and the heads soured before they dried. I dried mine in the oven of the cookstove. It was a lengthy process, and half the class lost interest. That's how I happen to make David, his mother, Aunt Betsy Trotwood, and someone else, who must not have been very important since I can't remember him. Twelve years old at the time, I tackled the project with a vengeance. I studied costumes of the period, practiced my English accent (which I did not get to use, because all the other voices were Southern), and learned that I had the responsibility of not only my own character, but of my other marionettes as well. Someone was always calling out, "Tom! Your marionette is tangled." That was the beginning of my acquiring patience.

How often have I wanted to express my gratitude to that art teacher for her understanding and encouragement. And to think I didn't even particularly like her at the beginning of that school year! She had the gift of seeing through timidity and immaturity, and succeeded in putting me on the path that led to my life's work.

The David Copperfield marionettes were exhibited at the Nashville Public Library, setting another pattern in my life; for that was the first of the many displays I have created for the Children's Division of the library.

In high school I did a playlet about the French court for a history class, and a scene from *The Lady of the Lake* for the English teachers at a state teachers' convention. I learned much more about history, and about Sir Walter Scott, than I would have otherwise. Puppetry knows no age or grade limitation.

I learned that I could be anyone, do anything, with the puppets to help me. I could forget my embarrassment because I was not seen.

At the age of twelve I had found my medium. With all the assurance

---

* *Marionettes, Masks and Shadows* by W. H. Mills and L. M. Dunn. (Garden City, N. Y.: Doubleday, Page & Co., 1927).

and inner knowledge of an adolescent dreamer, I knew I had the ability to create characters, to be a playwright, a scenic artist, a costume designer, an actor—nothing was beyond me. Happily no one told me differently. My only limitation was my imagination, and that knew no bounds.

I'll repeat my advice to teachers! Start out with hand puppets. They are so much fun that you may never go on to marionettes. I would not advise making marionettes with children below the fifth grade. The frustrations outweigh the joys. And before you puppeteers start rehearsing any play, play around with the puppets. Have fun improvising with them.

Puppets provide a spendid way for showing emotions. On sensitive hands puppets can live, but they demand more than your hands—you must give them your heart.

WITH PEOPLE IN PLAYS

Hand puppets seem to have an affinity for working with humans. The difference in size is no barrier to a good relationship. One word of advice to anyone who plans to talk to puppets: don't try for the last word. It is very difficult to top the lines of a puppet who knows what he is doing. When the human half of a team gracefully gives the spotlight to the puppet, the audience responds in a most sympathetic manner.

Several plays were done at the Nashville library with puppets and people acting together. In one, the queen was human and her two children were dogs wearing crowns. In the four months that the play ran not one person questioned the logic of the casting. The dog puppets behaved in a reasonable (and spoiled) way, and played their parts well. The play's the thing, no matter the casting.

A puppet can steal a scene from a human—sometimes without even trying. At times this is a real help, especially if the performance is beginning to drag. On the other hand, permitting a puppet to attract too much attention, when others onstage are doing something important, can ruin the scene. Even when the director isn't watching, the puppet should use good stage manners.

After doing several puppet-people plays, we took an informal poll of reactions. Most of the people questioned seemed to prefer the all-puppet shows. This led to one conclusion: an actor must be very good to work onstage with puppets. Unskilled performers cannot rise to this occasion. If you plan a play using both puppets and people, be certain that your actors are of real professional caliber.

IN MOVIES

Home movies are great fun, especially for the people in them, and for their immediate families. Everyone usually acts very silly, makes funny faces, and waves at the camera. Filming a puppet show can be a real challenge, whether it is done as a recreational project or as a classroom effort. If it is done well you will be proud to show it. And it doesn't take much more thought to do it well.

Plan the movie carefully. Be serious—perhaps sensible is a better word—because you really should enjoy the shooting. Each time you giggle and ruin a scene you waste film (and film costs money) that could be put to better use.

Try to shoot your first movie in proper sequence to make editing easy. Let your cameraman tell you exactly what he has framed. Then you will know where to place the action. Rehearse each scene while the camera follows it. Nothing is more disconcerting than to get a roll of film developed and discover that half the action is off camera.

You do not have to use a puppet booth when making a movie. The puppets can appear in all sorts of places—on tree limbs, in automobiles, on rooftops, as well as in their special settings. Keep the puppets active, but not frantic. Keep the plot simple. Select a very short story for your first movie. Make the action so clear that the story can be followed without dialogue.

After you have had a bit of experience, you can attempt something more elaborate. Try puppet spoofs of TV commercials. Puppets have a flair for satire. Avoid extreme close-ups unless your puppets are carefully made. Have just one director. Too many people giving orders only confuses everyone. The cameraman is the one who really has the last word in a movie. Be nice to him.

IT'S TRADITIONAL

The curtains close, the performance is over. For an hour my personality has been split many times over. Without this legitimate outlet I would surely go mad. Maybe I am mad and don't know it.

Could I stop puppeteering? Marco has a blank look on his face. I wonder if he knows? If he does I'll never find out. He doesn't talk to me.

Felicia is looking sternly through her nose glasses. I forgot to remove the safety pin that fastens the wig to her head. Sorry, old girl.

Could I give up puppetry? Certainly not. The show must go on. Why must the show go on? I gave Christopher Churchmouse the answer when someone asked why he lived in that poor, old church. He replied, "It's traditional, you know." And so it is.

(The End)

217

BIBLIOGRAPHY

Ackley, Edith Flack. *Marionettes: Easy to Make, Fun to Use*. Philadelphia: J. B. Lippincott Co., 1939.

Baird, Bill. *Art of the Puppet*. Boston: Plays, Inc., 1966.

Batchelder, Marjorie H. *Puppet Theatre Handbook*. New York: Harper & Bros., 1947.

Bramall, Eric, and Sommerville, Christopher C. *Expert Puppet Technique*. Boston: Plays, Inc., 1966.

Bufano, Remo. *Remo Bufano's Book of Puppetry*. New York: The Macmillan Co., 1950.

Ficklen, Bessie A. *Handbook of Fist Puppets*. Philadelphia: J. B. Lippincott Co., 1935.

Fraser, Peter. *Introducing Puppetry*. New York: Watson-Guptill Publications, 1968.

McPharlin, Paul. *Puppet Theatre in America*. Boston: Plays, Inc., 1969.

Mills, Winifred H., and Dunn, Louise M. *Marionettes, Masks and Shadows*. Garden City: Doubleday, Page & Co., 1927.

Philpott, A. R. *Modern Puppetry*. Boston: Plays, Inc., 1967.

Rutter, Vicki. *A B C Puppetry*. Boston: Plays, Inc., 1969.

Tichenor, Tom. *Folkplays for Puppets You Can Make*. Nashville: Abingdon Press, 1959.

Wall, L. V.; White, G. A.; and Philpott, A. R. *Puppet Book*. Boston: Plays, Inc., 1950.

Worrell, Estelle Ansley. *Be a Puppeteer: The Lively Puppet Book*. New York: McGraw-Hill Co., 1969.

Index

(Note: Among the photographs in *Tom Tichenor's Puppets* are some which are from plays not included in the book. The pictures are shown to give the reader an idea of the Tichenor costumes, stage settings, or theaters. Those photographs are included in the following index; other illustrations are indexed only when it would appear to be an added convenience for the reader.)

Designer:	*Giorgetta Bell*
Type:	*Bodoni Book, 12 pt., leaded 2 pts.*
Typesetter:	*Parthenon Press*
Manufacturer:	*Parthenon Press*
Printing Process:	*Offset*
Paper:	*70# Reference Opaque*
Binding:	*Columbia Fictionette, Natural Finish*
	FNV—3422—Blue